THE 9 STEPS TO
EMOTIONAL
FITNESS

A TOOL-KIT FOR LIFE
IN THE 21ST CENTURY

WARREN REDMAN

Merlin Star Press, Calgary

Merlin Star Press
Calgary, Canada

National Library of Canada Cataloguing in Publication Data

Redman, Warren
        The 9 steps to emotional fitness: a tool-kit for life in the 21st century / Warren Redman.

Includes bibliographical references and index.
ISBN 0-9699189-1-7

1. Self actualization (Psychology) 2. Success--Psychological aspects. 3. Interpersonal relations. I. Title. II. Title: Nine steps to emotional fitness.
BF637.S4R435 2002   158   C2002-911373-3

Printed in Canada by Acorn Graphics Ltd.

Dedication

This book is dedicated to the memory of Carol Montgomery and Lin Kreis, and to the hundreds of other students, colleagues and friends who have accompanied me on the journey to Emotional Fitness and Inner Balancing.

Acknowledgements

Writing a book is essentially a lone occupation. I have received support and encouragement from many along the way. My special thanks go to Marianne Kuttner for the wonderful illustrations, to Carla Pelkey for her cover design and content layout, to Allan Webner for sending me some great quotes, and to Carolyn Koltutsky and Fred Klein for their valuable, if sometimes painful, comments on my manuscripts. Above all, I want to thank my wonderful and lovely wife, Nicole Tremblay, for her belief in me, her unflagging support and the love that has helped bring this book into being.

Other books by Warren Redman

Support for Volunteers (1977) The Volunteer Centre, UK

Working Towards Independence (1979) West-Central, UK

Finding your Own Support (1982) NAYC, UK

Creative Training (1982) NAYC, UK

Help! Finding and Keeping Volunteers (1983) NAYC, UK

Partners (1985) Northamptonshire County Council, UK

Listening Power (1988) Management Learning Resources, UK

Show What You Know (1989) NYB, UK

Portfolios for Development (1994) Kogan Page, UK & Nichols
     Publishing, USA

Achieving Personal Success (1995) Merlin Star Press, Canada

Counselling Your Staff (1995) Kogan Page, UK
     Portuguese Translation by Clio Editora, Brazil

Facilitation Skills for Team Development (1996) Kogan Page, UK
     Portuguese Translation by Clio Editora, Brazil

Our enquiry has led us to the heart of being.

Jean-Paul Sartre
Being and Nothingness

Then a woman said, Speak to us of Joy and Sorrow.
And he answered:
Your joy is your sorrow unmasked.

Kahlil Gibran
The Prophet

CONTENTS

INTRODUCTION
LET ME OUT OF HERE

*To be what we are, and
to become what we are
capable of becoming,
is the only end in life.*

Robert Louis Stevenson
(1850 -1894), Writer

Deep inside you the real you is trying to get out and connect with others. Once, maybe years ago, you were authentically, wonderfully you. Then something happened. You grew up and in the process your essential self became swamped in a morass of other people's egos.

It is no coincidence that you hold this book in your hand. You are ready to experience great relationships and to become emotionally fitter than you have ever been. What happens when you are emotionally fit? Your life, your relationships, your career and your general health become the best they can be. You become free from fear and live the life you dreamed, even if nothing around you changes.

The horrific events of September 11th 2001, within a few months after they happened, became simply a blip on the radar screen of human consciousness. While all of us who watched the pictures of the plane exploding into the second of the twin towers have them indelibly imprinted into our brains, the long term impact on our emotions is more subtle. After the immediate shock and the knee-jerk reactions of politicians, millions of people were asking themselves questions that have yet to be answered. Questions like, "if life can be ended like that, how can I make mine more meaningful?" Later, other kinds of questions emerged such as, "how can some people be so angry and frustrated that they resort to acts of violence like this?" As the outward expressions of fear and confusion subside into inner conflicts a third type of question emerges; "what can I do to make things better?"

The journey into our emotions, into 'inner space' is possibly the last great journey left for humankind. It is certainly the most important ever taken. Imagine if we were all secure within ourselves, were able to be authentic and at the same time take full responsibility for our own actions. Imagine if we understood and could articulate our deepest wishes and treat ourselves and others with the same honourable respect. Just imagine. This is the journey that I have travelled for the past thirty years. This is the belief and the imagination that has drawn me to work with others on their own journeys of self-discovery. One step at a time this world can become a better place. It can be fun, and the most enjoyable experience of your life. It can sometimes be a long, hard and rocky journey fraught with disappointments and setbacks. Is it worth it? Ask anyone who has taken the road less travelled and you will know that it is. The beauty and the revelations along the way make it so. When will the journey end? Hopefully never, and you will be paving the way for others as you open up more possibilities for yourself. Along the way your relationships will blossom as never before and you are likely to feel and have the success you desire.

The remarkable stories of most people's lives hardly ever get told or seen as remarkable. Once you start to listen to those stories you begin to recognize something. You begin to see that the people you thought you knew are far more than you ever imagined. What you have been seeing is the outer manifestation of all the layers that have masked the real person inside. When you hold out your hand to reach inside you find a being that has experiences, emotions, ideas and dreams that will amaze you. Even more amazing is the recognition when it comes, that you too have an inner story with the potential to inspire others just as much as any Everest climber. Everest has always been there waiting, or so some would say to be climbed. The metaphor of the highest peak in the world is often used to show us the achievements of others and how it is possible to overcome the greatest challenges of our life. Most of us more familiar with the mundane challenges of everyday life may not easily make the connection with ourselves, yet the stories I have heard of the inner journeys made by apparently otherwise unremarkable people have made the scaling of Everest seem almost irrelevant. It is the uniqueness of each journey, of each inner discovery and each personal achievement that is its true value. For the true value of each life is in its own unique experience.

FOUR STORIES

Throughout this book I will refer to the stories of people with whom I have had the pleasure and honour to work during the past twenty years. I have not used their real names and have obscured details to avoid recognition. If you think that you recognize someone or that I am talking about you it is because although each of us is a unique individual, we mostly share the same universal human experiences and emotions that accompany them.

Ϙ

Maureen had a naturally infectious laugh and displayed a deeply caring nature for others. Yet she was troubled and hardly knew why. Nor could she find a way of saying how she felt to anyone else. She would sit at home alone and meditate, feeling a foreboding of something evil, forcing herself to put those feelings out of her mind as she concentrated on more positive thoughts. She was highly successful in her work as an engineer, although it did not satisfy her as much as she thought it should. She was fearful of establishing an intimate relationship or of sharing herself in any way.

Her personal journey began one evening when she came into an Emotional Fitness group. It was a tremendous, almost terrifying challenge for Maureen simply being with others who were exploring aspects of themselves. It brought up fears that she had been fighting for years, fears that were unknown, and that she knew had been a part of her all her life.

Two of Maureen's qualities are courage and intelligence. She knew that she had touched on something that was vitally important to her healthy survival. She felt safe enough in the group environment to know that this was a place where she might at last face her fears, make sense of and overcome them.

A year later, Maureen cast off her fears, emerged as a happier, more vibrant woman whose laughter is now as authentic as her caring nature. She is now in a long-term and delightful relationship in which she feels she can constantly grow. She has given up her job and is now running her own successful healing practice. She is totally at home within groups of people to the extent that she is now teaching what she has learned.

Ϙ

The first time that Jim came into a group, he was at the lowest ebb of his life. His relationship was breaking up and he had no idea why or what he could do about it. His career as a scientific analyst was on the line. He felt that he had been treated unfairly and that this had dogged him all his life. Most of the time that he took to talk about his plight he was in tears – a big man sobbing his heart out.

Six months later Jim's relationship is better than it has ever been. More significantly Jim is emotionally stronger and clearer about himself than he has been in his life. He is now using what he has learned about himself to help others to discover themselves. He has recently been promoted to team leader in his work.

The less I know that I know, the wiser I become.

Q

Claudette was drawn to an Emotional Fitness course because she sensed that it was the right time for her. With a delightfully wicked sense of humour, a sharp insight and a desire to have everything clear and organized Claudette felt some dismay when she began to feel more confused rather than clearer. Claudette had been searching for an answer for years in relationships, in work, on courses and retreats. Yet she had never known what the question was. In the group, she felt listened to, learned to listen to others and finally learned to hear herself. She discovered that her quest was for inner peace and a sense of wisdom and that her question was "when and how did I lose my peace and my wisdom?"

Claudette is now one of the most peaceful people I know, and in a happy and fulfilled relationship with the man who is now in her life and more importantly, with herself. She engages her wisdom by passing it on to others.

Q

Greg is regarded by many people who know him as a wise guide and teacher, and a man who has a deep understanding of himself and others. It was not always so. Greg had been working on that understanding for some years, yet still felt enormous frustration in his life when he came into a group about a year ago. He was highly regarded in his profession and had a successful career. He had experienced a damaging divorce and was finding the day-to-day separation from his children hard to bear. He felt guilty, unhappy, confused, and unable to express himself when he needed to.

Greg is now in a wonderful relationship, and has discovered the happy, inquisitive, wise self that was always within him, but that he had driven out because he listened to voices other than his own that told him he was not OK. He is discovering a new passion in his life's work and is now an inspiration and a mentor to a growing number of people.

These four people have all experienced the transformations that take place when we embark upon and continue our Emotional Fitness journeys.

I can sum up my own story in seven words. ***I used to have an unhappy childhood.***

Not only can we change our lives in the present and the future, we can even change our lives in the past. How is that possible? In *The 9 Steps to Emotional Fitness*, we will accompany these people and others on their own journeys. You will also be able to try some Emotional Fitness exercises for yourself. I will share with you the process of Inner Balancing. You will have the opportunity to explore parts of yourself that will surprise and delight you.

Even if you do not have the chance to take part in the 12-week Emotional Fitness course you can spend that time learning Inner Balancing with the help of this book. If you have the good fortune to join a course you can work though all the nine steps with a trained Emotional Fitness Instructor.

During this journey, you will learn something about Inner Balancing, its philosophy and background and how it relates to some of the psychotherapeutic approaches of the past. This is the groundwork that will give you the tools to become authentically you in relationship with others. I will explain the background to Inner Balancing, which has its roots in the work of Freud and the psychoanalytical approach, Jung and his Universal Symbols, Carl Rogers and the Person Centred approach, Eric Berne and Transactional Analysis, Fritz Perls and *Gestalt* Therapy and finally Eugene Heimler and Human Social Functioning. Inner Balancing is a synthesis of the best parts of those teachings laced with my own experience of life, including the healing and developmental processes that have proved to be the best for me in terms of positive results.

THE ROAD TO DISCOVERY

The search for meaning is as old as humanity. It is partly what defines human beings as distinct from other forms of life on earth. The search has been through spiritual growth and understanding, and the search for deities and stories that explain the universe and the human condition. Ancient philosophies and systems developed prayer and reflection, meditation and ritual. In every society and every age since humans have left their mark, there is evidence of this search for meaning. We are all affected in some way now, whether at a conscious or unconscious level by the beliefs and stories of the Hebrews, of the ancient Greeks, of Eastern philosophers, of the Aboriginals of the Americas and the South Pacific and the tribes of Africa, of the religions of Judaism, Hinduism, Islam, Christianity, Buddhism and many others.

As a child I was fascinated with characters like the young shepherd boy David who single-handedly defeated the giant Goliath with a slingshot and thereby helped the Hebrews conquer the Philistines. I recall trying to make a slingshot with a piece of bandage and a pebble. It never worked well and I missed my target and the whole point of the story. But that didn't matter at the time. What I construed at a deeper level was that I might not be as

When all is said and done, there's a lot more said than done.

insignificant as I thought I was. After all, if David could do that and later on become king of Israel, didn't it mean that I might get to be someone of significance? The stories and symbology of Jesus left me with one important message, that of loving your neighbour as yourself. I had no idea what that meant. Loving myself was not something I could grasp. How could I love my neighbours? I didn't even know them! Yet love as a concept stayed with me until, through a process of awakening what had been dormant for so long, I discovered it as a reality within myself. After bible stories I read the tales of the Greek mythological heroes and journeyed with them in my childhood fantasies. Did I understand the significance? Not at all. But I must have absorbed something into my sub-consciousness, since my search for the Golden Fleece of the mysterious inner self has been in its own way, just as epic a journey. An uncle gave me the poems of Omar Khayyam when I was about eleven years old. The impact on me was enormous. I struggled to understand the meaning of the words because I knew that they were telling me something important. I had a glimmer even then that the answers to my unformulated but painful questions were to be found, not from outside me, but from within.

Joseph Campbell who studied myths and how they reveal our own inner mysteries to us tells the story of a tigress who, pregnant and weak with hunger came across a herd of goats. She chased one of them, but exhausted she collapsed and gave birth to a baby tiger before she died. The goats came back to investigate and following their maternal instincts, cared for the tiger cub, which was brought up believing he was a goat. He ate grass, which was bad for his digestive system, bleated and grazed quietly with the other goats. A couple of years later another tiger attacked the herd and was surprised to come across the spectacle of a weak-looking tiger among the scattering goats. The big tiger took the youngster to a pond and showed him his reflection. "See, you're a tiger. You don't eat grass and you don't bleat. Now eat this meat." The young tiger protested timidly, but forced some meat down himself and was surprised when he blurted out a roar.

The story is one that shows how we might see ourselves, surrounded and absorbed by our community as goats when we are really tigers. It takes reflection; it takes a new way of looking at things often with the help of someone wiser and more experienced than ourselves. It takes a different diet of understanding before we might get to recognize who we really are. Perhaps we are all tigers imagining that we are goats, because that is what we have been told we are. The problem is that as soon as we roar in the midst of goats they all run away. The secret is to be the tiger and keep it to yourself or to join with other tigers.

We are all products of the experiences, stories and beliefs that have permeated our personal environment even when some of those stories and beliefs are ancient and from other cultures. When we study the archetypes we may discover ourselves. Writing our own stories, exploring the myths of our own heritage and upbringing, is one of the most empowering and enlightening learning processes we can experience. The bridge between the ancient and modern, the philosophies of East and West, are to be found within the stories of our own lives ready to be rediscovered every day.

The later mainly Western dominated search for self began at the turn of the twentieth century with Sigmund Freud's development of psychoanalysis. While the analytic, purely interpretive approach of Freud may no longer be in vogue, and despite the now questionable approaches Freud employed with many of his patients, there is little doubt that much of what we know today of the human mind is derived from his pioneering work. Without Freud we would not now be aware of the unconscious and sub-conscious mind. Without his work we would not talk of the ego or of our repressed needs that may emerge in the form of addictive behaviours. Carl Jung took Freud's work in a different direction and gave us concepts of the collective unconscious, opening up the world of dreams and symbols. With Jung's interest in mythology and stories, it would not have escaped him that the earliest recorded dream analyst was Joseph of the Old Testament who interpreted the dreams of Pharaoh, and thereby saved the Egyptians and surrounding tribes from starvation during seven years of drought. Jung helped us to see that we can all be our own Joseph making sense of our dreams and therefore of ourselves. In the second half of the twentieth century a new breed of 'people explorers' emerged to point the way to a more self-empowering approach in understanding ourselves. The names of those who have affected me and my work the most are Carl Rogers, Eric Berne, Fritz Perls and Eugene Heimler. There are many others of course, and many approaches. The work and writings of such apparently different personalities as Stephen Covey, Louise Hay and Deepak Chopra lend much to the approaches that are included within Inner Balancing. Some of the wonderful teachers and mentors I had were people who never published anything of note, nor developed any

The point of life may just be to experience it.

specifically named process. The first four I have named however, were pioneers who helped to transform the lives of millions in a way that fits in with my philosophy of personal growth and self-empowerment. All of these teachers were moving away from the purely analytical, medical model of 'treating' people who were therefore labeled as 'sick'. Most therapies, even so-called holistic ones, still tend towards the assumption that there is something wrong with people that needs to be put right. Inner Balancing, based as it is on the pioneering work of those I have mentioned, and my own experiences and beliefs, is an approach that sees people as inherently fine, although they may from time to time be emotionally out of balance.

Carl Rogers developed what he called the person-centred approach. Rogers was a psychotherapist who believed that his clients, not he, knew how to heal themselves. He valued empathy as the most important quality he could offer, along with the belief that he needed to be congruent in his words and his actions with people. I was in my early thirties when I saw Carl Rogers at work as part of my own training. It was a delightful and rewarding experience and left an indelible mark on me. It showed me the importance of being fully attentive when the intention is to assist in a healing and developmental process. It showed me to leave my ego at the door when with a client I was counselling. It showed me the gift of humility in understanding that the client, not I, was the expert on his or her life. More than anything it showed me that the most important attribute of any helper is to have love in your heart. In *Becoming Partners*, Rogers wrote:

"We each commit ourselves to working together on the changing process of our present relationship, because that relationship is currently enriching our love and our life and we wish it to grow. I will risk myself by endeavoring to communicate any persisting feeling, positive or negative, to my partner – to the full depth that I understand it myself – as a living, present part of me. Then I will risk further by trying to understand with all the empathy I can bring to bear, his or her response, whether it is accusatory and critical or sharing and self-revealing. We will live by our own choices, the deepest organismic sensings of which we are capable, but we will not be shaped by the wishes, the rules, the roles which others are all too eager to thrust upon us. Perhaps I can discover and come closer to more of what I really am deep inside feeling, sometimes angry or terrified, sometimes loving and caring, occasionally beautiful and strong or wild and awful without hiding these feelings from myself. Perhaps I can come to prize myself as the richly varied person that I am. Perhaps I can openly be more of this person.

If so, I can live through my own experienced values, even though I am aware of all of society's codes. Then I can let myself be all this complexity of feelings and meanings and values with my partner, be free enough to give of love and anger and tenderness as they exist in me. Possibly then I can be a real member of the partnership, because I am on the road to being a real person. And I am hopeful that I can encourage my partner to follow his or her own road to a unique personhood, which I would love to share."

Carl Rogers showed the way. He wrote much about his work; what he left as a mystery for me was just how he could be as successful in helping others to find themselves in such a powerful way. Rogers helped to move psychotherapy away from the notion that 'doctor knows best' and from an analytic, medical model towards a more humanistic, person-centred one where the client has more control over his or her own healing.

Transactional Analysis (T.A.) was developed by Eric Berne as a way of providing a framework and a language that would help make psychiatry more accessible to people. Berne had observed the changes that are evident when individuals experience different emotions: the lawyer who in therapy acted and looked like a small boy, the teen who changed from a disgruntled rebel to a joyful child in a moment of changed circumstance. He wondered what was going on and created the concept of Adult, Parent and Child, giving those words definitions more to do with our emotional ego states than with the physical ages and roles of those people. This meant that we could all begin to recognize our own and others' behaviours when in those states. What caught the imagination of millions of aficionados of Transactional Analysis were the games that Berne recorded in his book *Games People Play*, games like 'Ain't It Awful', 'It's All You', 'Husbands Are Awful', and 'Poor Me'. Much laughter was heard, but the games are serious and the laughter was probably from embarrassed recognition. What we learned from Berne is that communication (or transactions) between people may be analyzed in terms of Parent, Adult or Child and that when the transaction is crossed (e.g. a simple Adult request gets a petulant Child or a disparaging Parent response), then the sense of being 'not OK' may be reinforced. So when you ask a close friend if he has seen your car keys and he answers, "don't tell me you've lost them", you may feel less than good about yourself and angry with him. He is being a Parent and you have returned to being a Child in that moment. T.A.

Love doesn't come with an "if".

has been an immensely helpful and popular approach assisting hundreds of thousands of people to make sense of what is going wrong in their communications and responses.

Gestalt is more of a philosophical belief than a specific therapeutic approach, although the psychotherapist Fritz Perls was a prime mover in integrating it into a psychological model. It helped many to confront themselves through accepting accountability for their behaviour and their lives, and through seeing that their perception of the world was a reflection of themselves. This challenged much of the universality of some of the previous approaches in favour of a more individualized response. In dreams, for example, rather than the symbols being capable of interpretation according to generally understood meanings, the dreamer has to make sense of the meanings personally by imagining each symbol as a part of the dreamer's inner self. In the sixties and early seventies, I participated in many *gestalt* groups. I observed that those who benefitted from them were already in a place of relatively high self-esteem, and able to handle the 'in-your-face' approach that challenges people to take full responsibility for their feelings and actions. Those who felt relatively insecure found the process too much to handle, and often left feeling even less self-assured. While recognizing that everyone will be in a unique stage of readiness for any personal growth, I believe that any approach needs to work wherever people are and challenge them at the pace that is a stretch without it being a breaking point.

Much of the learning I gained was through the Tavistock Institute for Human Relations in London, England. Great teachers and pioneers offered insights into the understanding of human development. The work of psychiatrist Scott Peck was of great interest to me. His discussion of love and spiritual growth in *The Road Less Travelled* brings clarity and a new understanding that has inspired millions. He writes:

"Since I am human and you are human, to love humans means to love myself as well as you. To be dedicated to human spiritual development is to be dedicated to the race of which we are a part, and this therefore means dedication to our own development as well as "theirs." Indeed, as has been pointed out, we are incapable of loving another unless we love ourselves, just as we are incapable of teaching our children self-discipline unless we ourselves are self-disciplined. It is actually impossible to forsake our own spiritual development in favor of someone else's. We cannot forsake self-discipline and at the same time be disciplined in our care for another. We cannot be a source of strength unless we

nurture our own strength."

Eugene Heimler was one of a breed of psychotherapists who drew from his own experience as much as from his scholarship. Heimler, known to his friends as John, survived the trauma of the concentration camps of Nazi Germany. He writes in the start of his book *Survival in Society*:

> *"My interest in the relationship of satisfaction and frustration as experienced by the individual and in his ability to turn pain to good account began when I was placed in Buchenwald, Auschwitz and other extermination camps as a young man of twenty-two, during the Second World War. ...My own emotional survival, I believe, was due to two main factors: first, that somehow I was able to draw on love received in the past, and second, my belief that, in order to be able to move towards the future, I had to do something about my dangerous predicament. I made an attempt to escape from the concentration camp and when I did so, although I exposed myself to very grave risks of being killed, the ghosts of the inner world disappeared. Meaning and action, therefore, seem to have played an important part in maintaining my survival and in my remaining alive."*

I was lucky enough to have become a student, a colleague and a friend of John Heimler. The approach he developed is called Human Social Functioning and provides a form and a structure to creative transformation. Through HSF, I began to discover how everything I had ever experienced in life and in my training came together in a glorious synthesis of understanding. The mystery of Carl Roger's talent for listening was unlocked. The language of Transactional Analysis became more meaningful. The power of *gestalt* offered new possibilities. John Heimler's HSF approach was the most empowering and useful process I had ever seen and experienced in my twenty years of exploration.

During the eighties and nineties a multitude of self-assessment tests have been devised and promoted so that we can all analyze ourselves and each other, becoming more knowledgeable about personality types, expected responses, preferred learning styles and how to fix ourselves. We have been fed a diet of 'how to' self-management books that creates an atmosphere and an expectation that simply by taking the advice of the expert we can become the person we want to be. Millions of people will purchase a book on how to become a millionaire in six months, thereby ensuring that the

We can all win the human race.

author becomes one. The search seems to be to become like someone else, to have the success of that person or the looks of this one, the confidence of him or the courage displayed by her.

Through Inner Balancing I have drawn from the best I have learned and experienced, bringing a greater accessibility to those who want to heal and develop themselves and a greater clarity to the mystique of the multitude of techniques, self-evaluation tests, systems and therapies that threaten to engulf us all. Inner Balancing is offered as a simple set of nine processes or steps that will help you to tell your stories, listen to yourself and take the journey to your own self fulfillment leading you to the relationships, success and balance you want in your life.

The first Inner Balancing step is the one that is the foundation for everything else. It is **Listening Power**, the power to listen more deeply to others and to yourself than you believed possible. You can also teach others to listen to you in the way that you want. You will need to spend some time on this so that you become confident in your ability before you go on. Most people like to think that they are good at listening. Since you are reading this I'm guessing that you are better than most. Listening Power will enable you to listen more deeply than you ever imagined.

The second step we will take is **Learning from Experience**. Your portfolio of experience will be the gateway for you to discover more about your experiences and what you have learned from them. The combination of Listening Power with Learning from Experience is going to bring you personal insights that have been hidden from you even though you have always known about them. One of the things that you will discover is that you know everything you need to know about yourself already. In fact you have probably known as much as you need to since you were about four years old. Inner Balancing will allow you to uncover that knowledge. You will find no answers in Inner Balancing or within the covers of these pages. You will find the questions, the guidelines for you to discover your answers, and eventually the question to help you find your own questions. Your discoveries will be unique to you. Nobody else could have created them. Learning from Experience is one of the ways for you to make these discoveries.

The third step is the one that gives Inner Balancing its name. The **Lifescale** will help you to discover the emotional balance you have in your life and how you can get to change that balance if you desire. The Lifescale is the key that will unlock the door to your understanding of what brings you satisfaction and frustration. There are ten questions, each of them opening you to a discovery of a piece of your emotional self. When you have explored all ten questions and found the connections between your answers, you will make sense of why you feel what you feel and how you can begin to transform some of those frustrations into satisfactions.

The fourth step that you will take is the **Time Capsule**. Now you will start to connect your present self with your past and even your future. This is when you get to meet your essential self, the person you always knew you were. You will discover that you can become your own guru, your own personal guide. The Time Capsule is a powerful though sometimes difficult process and one that will provide you with the basic material to become who you really are. It can also be a source of great creativity, fun and delight as you and your inner child get to meet each other. Once you have a great relationship with your past and future self, you will open the door to better relationships with others.

The fifth step of Inner Balancing is the one in which you get to practice the Listening Power skills you have gained within a group of people. This is called the **Group Dialogue**. You can use it at work, in the Boardroom, with family, with friends or in any group wanting to share thoughts and ideas or deal with problems in a healthy way. Through this process you will gain a new perspective on how to communicate, and especially how to listen and help others listen to each other.

The sixth step is simply **Storytelling,** Inner Balancing style. This storytelling is a way for you to access your own inner stories and to gain greater understanding of yourself, not only in the past, but also now. In combination with what you will have learned about yourself from the Time Capsule, your stories will help you transform the past, as a way of making your life in the present and the future more fulfilling.

In **Dreamtime**, the seventh step of Inner Balancing, you will learn to access your dreams in a different and powerful way, enabling you to understand your own meanings from the symbols you have created in your dreams and to make sense of what you are telling yourself.

The Mirror is the eighth step and one that will bring you face-to-face with yourself. Having taken the other seven steps you will be ready for this and delighted with the results. You will be seeing the new you emerge. The conversation that ensues could be the most productive you have ever had.

Your secret life is safe with those who love you.

The ninth and final step is called **Connections** in which you will use a personal symbol to help you to connect with all that you have been learning and enable you to move forward to achieve long lasting emotional fitness.

The whole of Inner Balancing can therefore be seen as a series of interconnected and integrated steps that combine into a continual life process of self-discovery, transformation and manifestation of who we really are. In this way we transcend who we have become – a product of our environment and experiences – to being more authentically ourselves. When this happens we are emotionally fit and live a life of personal fulfillment.

A CONTRACT FOR EMOTIONAL FITNESS

Before going on I invite you to create your own personal learning contract. The reason for this will become clear very soon. This contract is between you and yourself. It is the vital first step to help you to create more Emotional Fitness in your life in the best way possible. This is a partnership. It won't work without you. It would be like going to the gym and standing on the sidelines watching other people work out in the hope of become more physically fit. Even when you decide to become involved your personal trainer will help you to figure out what your specific needs are before you launch into a workout session.

In preparation consider what Emotional Fitness means to you. Here are a few ideas. Feel free to make notes, add to or amend mine as you wish. You will need to have your journal or a notebook that you will reserve for this purpose.

Emotional Fitness is:
- choosing your reactions to people and situations
- coping with pressure in a way that doesn't leave you feeling stressed
- freeing yourself from addictive behaviours
- feeling OK, even when things go wrong
- expressing yourself honestly without needing to put anyone down
- being authentic without worrying about how others see you
- trusting yourself without judging others
- asking for what you want without being attached to the outcome
- listening to others without getting in the way
- understanding and accepting yourself fully
- living your life right now the way you want
- and...

Make your own notes now. ✐▭

Your personal learning contract is renegotiable at any time and we will revisit it regularly to make sure either that you are staying on track or that you revise what you are seeking for yourself when that becomes clearer. In fact, part of the beauty of this journey is that as you become clearer, and as you satisfy some of the initial requirements that you have for yourself, you can move on to other, maybe far more ambitious and profound personal goals.

Here are the personal learning contracts of Maureen, Jim, Claudette and Greg.

> *Maureen: I want to learn to be myself. I want to discover my purpose and to find a way of expressing myself in my work that is more meaningful to me.*

> *Jim: I want to improve my relationships, with my wife and children, and especially with myself. I want to learn to listen more.*

> *Claudette: I need to create more peace in my life. I don't want to have to feel in control all the time. I'd like to reach a state of wisdom.*

> *Greg: I want to deal with my feelings of guilt, and change some of my negative self-beliefs into positive ones. I want to listen to myself more and not just follow other people's expectations of me.*

The personal learning contracts were developed during individual interviews with me, each lasting an hour. The statements that they wrote and that you have just read were the result of much thought and exploration into feelings. My role was to help them to get to the essence, the inner meanings of what they had said during our time together in that initial interview.

If you do not have someone to listen to you, here are the stages in the development of your personal Emotional Fitness learning contract:

1. Settle yourself into a relaxed frame of mind. Have a pen or pencil and your notebook handy and enough light for you to write with ease. Make yourself comfortable. Close your eyes and take three deep breaths, taking your time and being aware of your own breathing. Notice any tension in you and make a conscious choice to relax as much you can.
2. Ask yourself the question: what commitment do I want to make to myself in terms of being emotionally fit? Think about this for a few minutes, then

Put your buts into a can.

start to jot down some of the key words that come to mind. Whatever you write now will be perfect. If you doubt this, you already have a start. When you are ready, write down those key words. You may find two or three or up to twelve. ᴑ◄☰

3. Using those words, put together a statement that says what you are seeking for yourself. This will probably include what you believe is not working for you, negative feelings that you would like to change, vague or clear notions of what it is that you want from life that is different from your experience of it now. ᴑ◄☰

4. If you have written more than fifty words, read what you have written and condense it into no more than fifty, and preferably no more than thirty words. This summary will be the essence of what you are seeking for yourself at this point. Remember that you can always change or develop this as you go along. Write your personal learning contract now. ᴑ◄☰

5. Now reflect on how you tackled this task. Was it easy or difficult? Did you feel anxious about getting it 'right' or that you won't be able to achieve what you want? Do you feel skeptical about the whole thing? Are you excited, bored, panicking, impatient, comfortable or…whatever else? Write down how you reacted. ᴑ◄☰

6. Finally, now that you have reflected on your reactions and what you have learned, look again at your personal learning contract making any changes or additions that you want keeping it still to a maximum of fifty words. ᴑ◄☰

Congratulations! You have begun your journey. Welcome to the world of Inner Balancing.

PERSONAL INFLUENCES

Next, reflect on and recognize the main influences that have helped you to learn more about yourself so far. Like the influences I have described in this chapter you will have found teachers, stories, mentors in your life. Perhaps a parent or other relative or friend inspired you. Think of books you have read, movies you have seen, a poem or song that moved your spirit and perhaps changed something or rather drew out something new in you.

1. Remember to relax first. Get yourself in the mood and the right space for this. If you are used to meditation this will be natural to you; otherwise be conscious of how you feel. Notice your breathing and any tension in your body. The purpose of this is for you to become ever more aware of your

true self.

2. Now write down as much as you can about the most important positive influences on your own personal development. ◑◀▤

3. Reviewing what you have written, give some thought to the key theme or themes arising from these influences. In other words, what was it about those influences that had such an impact on you? This will help you to discern what you most believe in and are drawn to in your own quest in life. ◑◀▤

You have now completed your preparation for the journey. This has been like packing your bags, checking that you have the tickets, that your passport is in order and you know where you are off to, although no idea of what awaits you. I hope you are excited, but of course you may be anything but. I can offer to you only these processes, these nine steps of Inner Balancing, since they are what I believe to be the most effective and powerful ones for our own emotional fitness and personal fulfillment. Since you are unique and therefore different from me, you will experience Inner Balancing in your own way.

The moment of truth comes anytime you want to hear it.

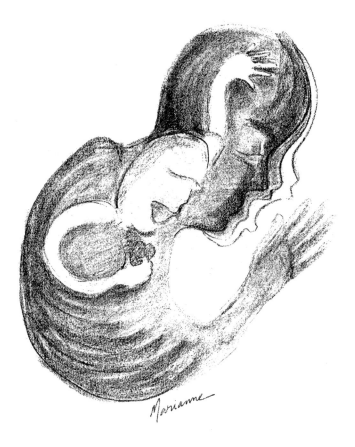

STEP 1: LISTENING POWER
IS ANYONE OUT THERE?

Listen or thy tongue
will keep thee deaf.

Native American Proverb

Two great talkers will
not travel far together.

Spanish Proverb

I want to share this immediate experience with you. Here I am staring at the blank page on the computer screen wondering how to start, hearing in my head a string of thoughts and words, none of which seem to do justice to what I want to say. Now, having started I realize that I am beginning to relax and words are flowing because I am listening to myself. What I am hearing is that I can simply write down my current experience and my immediate thoughts and feelings. Wow, this is liberating! When I listen to myself things actually begin to happen. Best of all, I can express myself. This stuff works!

Now that I have unblocked myself through using what I know to be the most powerful tool for self-understanding and growth available, we can move on, for this is exactly what this book and Emotional Fitness is all about – how we can fully listen to ourselves and each other. Imagine that, when you are blocked you can simply listen to what is going on within you, change the feeling, take the action you need and get on with life – you can even help someone else to do the same. What an effect this would have on your and others' ability to feel more positive, to have greater clarity or greater understanding even about the uncertainties, to feel free to take the decisions that have been difficult and to act in a way that is authentic. Imagine how this would change work, relationships, life itself. Imagine how this could liberate the human spirit.

I discovered for myself the real power of listening some years after I had embarked on a career that included community development and counselling work. As many people do, I believed that I was a good listener. Was that not why people came to me to seek out my guidance and support? My years of training at such places as the Tavistock Institute for Human Relations in London and my practical development work with communities, groups and individuals brought me to a meeting with Professor Eugene (John) Heimler. My serious understanding of the power of listening began when I met him. It took another seven years before I was able to make sense of the actual process of listening that would become the foundation of Inner Balancing as I slowly developed it. What happened at that meeting with Heimler? Why did it take so long for me to understand it?

Another way to ask those questions is to ask, "how can something so simple as listening be so difficult?" What John Heimler did was to tell us that he would listen to us. There were four of us at this meeting with him to discuss a community project we were planning, and in which we seemed to have arrived at an impasse. He asked each of us in turn to say why we thought we were there. He asked a couple of questions. He made a summary of what he had heard. He asked each of us to say what we wanted to do. All of this took about forty minutes. It is hard to describe how I felt as we left Professor Heimler's house that first time. The description I have given is so mundane, so apparently simplistic that it seems hardly worth mentioning. Yet he had clearly done something that had a far-reaching impact on my three colleagues and me, and on the community project that we had been planning.

That is why it took me so long to figure out what had actually happened. The one thing I was certain of at the time was that I wanted to find out more and I wanted to learn from John Heimler what was so different about his approach because in the forty minutes we spent with him our group of four recognized with startling clarity for the first time what held us back and why the project was stalled. The details don't matter. What does matter is that all of my training up until that moment suddenly seemed to have been a background for what I needed to do. I didn't know it at the time, but this was to be the turning point in my own personal and professional life direction.

As I learned the processes and practice of Human Social Functioning and worked closely with John Heimler, I became more and more adept at using his Scale of Social Functioning and other methods with my own clients who came for counselling or coaching or personal development training. Mostly however, I learned through my own observation. What was Heimler doing that was so powerful? He did not believe in the need for the then fashionable, yet long drawn-out and inevitably expensive analytical form of therapy for his clients. He helped people arrive at their own understanding of, and conclusions to their own issues in four to six sessions, sometimes less. He enabled people to transform their negative experiences and beliefs into positive, creative action, faster and more lastingly than I believed possible. There was magic here and yet there were no tricks. This was real magic. I wanted to find out what this magic was and I wanted to go further with it. Not content with offering psychotherapy to individuals, my desire was to discover and then teach the tools for people to use for themselves, and to pass on to others in their lives. So I spent nine years working with and observing Heimler.

What did I observe? I observed someone listening. I observed that there were two main elements that enabled people to be listened to in such a powerfully positive way. The first element was that Heimler did not get in the way. Now it is important to understand that John Heimler was not a meek man. He was lively, with a deep sense of humour that spilled out of him. While he was compassionate he would always say exactly what he thought without fear. He loved to tell stories and seldom turned down any opportunity to share one from his wealth of experiences. His voice had a deep, rich timbre and this, linked with his Hungarian accent, attracted strong attention. Remember too, that his experience as a survivor from the death camps of war-torn Europe gave him a kind of invulnerability and a heroic quality that he would play on quite overtly when he wanted to. And yet when he listened to someone he did not get in the way. The reason he did not get in the way of anyone he was listening to was that he did not need to. And the reason he did not need to was that he had dealt with his own feelings of fear and pain and anguish and loss and other issues through his own psychotherapeutic work that was part of his own healing and part of his training.

The second element that I observed in Heimler's listening was that there was a clear structure. Seldom did he talk about this structure and never did I hear him give an explanation of it in any lecture or discussion. While he did hint at parts of it, it appeared as though what he was doing was almost intuitive rather than thought out. I noticed that the same process was going on consistently and that it had a clear structure.

Inner Balancing has as its most important tool, the structure for listening that I observed and tried to make sense of and now offer in my training and through this book. I call it Listening Power. As to how you will learn to get out of the other person's way when you want to listen to them; when you

There are four L's in life: love, laughter, listening and learning.

get to know and understand yourself more through the pages of this book or on an Emotional Fitness training course you will be listening to yourself enough to know that you no longer need to fight for attention, however subtly or unconsciously you may have been doing that.

Remember Jim who was in the depth of despair and who believed his relationship to be breaking up? One of the key difficulties he had was in being able to listen clearly to his partner, especially when he was feeling under duress. When Jim learned the structure of Listening Power he became so excited and adept that not only was he able to turn his relationship around, he also extended his listening capabilities into every facet of his life. Even more significant is his newly found ability to listen to himself.

STAGE ONE: SET A CONTRACT

Jim's almost instant success began as soon as he started to use the first part of the Listening Power structure. He declared that he would listen. He told his partner he would listen. He told his children he would listen. He told his associates at work that he would listen. He told his friends. More than that, Jim discussed with each of these people how he would like to listen to them, how much time they could have, how he wanted to understand what they were saying, and that he would do his best to respond in a way that was helpful to them. He asked them what they wanted and didn't want. When it was appropriate, he asked them to listen to him in the same way.

In other words, Jim developed a contract with each of these people, that made it clear that they could say what they wanted, and that he would pay them full attention and show that he was listening to them. Words like 'respect' and 'reflecting back' were agreed upon. People knew exactly where they were with him. They didn't have to worry about whether or not Jim would listen to them, or think he would interrupt them, or would shy away from what they wanted to say. Jim noticed almost immediately that the freedom he had felt when he first started the Emotional Fitness course was shown by others when he listened to them. In the first few minutes of setting a contract with the person he was to listen to, the openness and honesty he experienced from them touched him to his core. Jim recognized that he felt trusted more fully than he had been for many years. Feeling this helped him to listen even more closely. He was getting out of the way.

Jim had two great successes. The first was that his wife learned to trust him in a deeper way than she had been able to in the past. By saying to her that he would listen, and by agreeing to do so when she asked, and by following this up with the skills of Listening Power, Jim's wife found that it felt safe for her to share anything with him, and that he would not judge her, advise her what to do, or interrupt her with his own thoughts. The result was amazing to Jim. The listening, the communication and the understanding between he and his wife became mutual. The love that they had for each other blossomed, as it never had before.

The second main success for Jim was that in setting his own contract to listen to himself, he began to see that the career path he had followed for years was not, after all, the one that was satisfying to him. He found that, while it had been his choice at first, over the years it had become frustrating, and that he had developed new interests and skills that he could not use in his current profession. This led to him embarking on a new career journey that brought him back a feeling of adventure and real value.

Jim's story is not an unusual one and each of us will probably have our own unique experience of similar stories. The remarkable thing is how few people ever listen to themselves or to each other. It is remarkable because when listening begins the door opens to lasting and positive change of the kind that Jim experienced. It is also remarkable because it is easy to do well as long as we allow it.

The first step in listening is to say clearly that you will be listening. This may sound a somewhat circular tour, so I want to take a little time to examine it in more detail. In fact I cannot emphasize the point enough. Think what happens in most conversations. Two or more people are talking to each other. Probably it will be more accurate to say that they are talking at each other. Each is likely to be waiting for the other to get their point across before coming in with their own point. Sometimes they don't even wait. Observe the next time you are in one of these 'normal' conversations. Even when there is no interrupting there is probably the 'internal interruption' of the thought processes that get in the way of listening to what the speaker is saying. Someone is talking to you about the trouble they have been having with their car or the new project they just got offered at work, and the excitement and fear this has brought up or their child who got into a fight at school. While they are talking are you concentrating on them or are you rehearsing in your mind the car problems you have had to face or the situation you have at work, or the time your own kid or you got into a fight? Or, maybe you are thinking of the answers you could come up with to help them solve their problems. Then, when they have stopped talking you manage to

Next time you breathe, notice it is a miracle.

get in your own current experience. Do you notice that your listener is giving you full attention and helping you to think through what you are saying or do you find that they come in with their own stories and solutions? When you have been in such a conversation do you leave feeling that you have been really listened to? How do you know whether or not you have been heard and understood? Do you know if anybody cared?

Suppose that at the start of your next conversation the other person you were with said to you, "why don't I just listen to what you have to say for fifteen minutes, then maybe you will listen to me for fifteen and afterwards we can each say what we heard the other talk about?" Bizarre? Maybe, but when you try this you will discover that something happens. You will find yourself feeling listened to. You will feel yourself trusted when the other person shares with you.

This first of the five Listening Power stages is possibly the most unusual. Yet without it, it is hard for real listening to take place because there is no understanding that it will happen. Listening begins when a contract is established.

Why do I put such an emphasis on listening in the first place? Because I believe that listening opens the door to self-understanding, inner security, empowerment and ultimately the development of each individual to be the authentic, unique and greatest person he or she can be. In seemingly tiny ways, every time we listen something great happens. Relationships are transformed.

Every time a father really listens to his small son instead of telling him what he should be doing, the boy grows to become a little more confident, a little more understanding, a little more knowing that it is OK to express himself and his feelings, a little more able to see that men are patient and loving.

When a teacher listens to her student rather than criticizing her for turning in poor work, the student gets to feel less of a failure, more of a person worthy of attention, more motivated to continue with a challenge, more likely to seek support.

When a boss listens to an employee instead of giving instructions, the employee becomes more willing to offer ideas, to find creative solutions, to take initiatives and to play a full role in the team.

When husbands and wives, or partners in other committed relationships truly listen to each other instead of maintaining a conversational plateau of superficiality or a truce of silence, they will understand each other better, grow in each other's company and strengthen their connection as a couple, while developing as individuals.

All this listening starts with a contract. It is as easy as one person saying (or showing) that he or she wants to be listened to and the other saying,"yes, I'll listen."

It is as simple as that, and as hard as that. Jim, when he tried it, found it hard at first because it seemed awkward and false, because he didn't quite know how to set up a contract to listen, because he felt self-conscious and because he was still dealing with his own feelings of unfairness and uncertainty. What began to make it easier for Jim was when he recognized what was happening almost as soon as he told people that he would just listen to them. As they opened up to him he saw that he was trusted and respected. While he had believed himself to be worthy of trust and respect he had seldom witnessed the evidence of this. His self-confidence and self-esteem blossomed leading to his ability to listen even more effectively. By setting a contract to listen he set the scene not only for the other person to be heard and to be understood, but also to his own sense of worthiness.

When I start a counselling session or when I see that someone wants to be listened to I invariably make it clear what I will offer and I ask what the other person is seeking. In a counselling or coaching session the contract will be more formal and will have been partly prearranged. We will have agreed on a time, place and length and perhaps the number of sessions. We might also have explored the reason that the person wanted counselling or coaching. At the initial session I clarify my role, for example that I will listen, do my best to help the person to understand what they are saying, help them to discover within themselves the answers they have to their own questions and that my main desire is to empower people rather than to offer advice. I emphasize that I keep our conversation entirely confidential. If they want to know, I tell them about my background and credentials and something about the Inner Balancing processes that I use.

I then ask them to tell me what works best for them and what does not, at any time. I seldom take notes, but if I do I ask if they feel comfortable with this. The reason, by the way, that I do not take notes, is that I believe that to do so immediately takes away from the other person a feeling of being in control and reduces the sense of empowerment that counselling or any listening or other therapeutic and developmental process, is intended to achieve. When anyone takes notes in Inner Balancing it is the person being listened to.

Having no choice is always a personal option.

My own experience of what happens when you establish a contract to listen or be listened to is that the listening starts at that point, before anything is shared.

When Scott called me to book a counselling appointment we went through the major part of the contract over the telephone. He said that he wanted to find someone who would challenge him and that he also felt would understand him. "I want to be called on my B.S." is how he put it. We established a time and place, which would be in my office that I assured him offered privacy without disturbance. Knowing that he was calling from a cell phone, I asked him to make sure it would be turned off when we met. I told him that I would act as a mirror to him reflecting back what he shared with me and making sure that he understood himself better, and that I would not be giving him advice or 'fixing' him. He responded that that was just what he was seeking and that he'd "had enough advice and fixing to last him a life-time." It seemed like we had a deal.

> *When Scott arrived for his first session his first words were: "You know, since we spoke on the phone I gave a lot of thought to what I wanted to discuss. It's almost as though I was here already. I know there's more, but it seems like I have sorted out some big things in my own mind."*
>
> *What Scott had experienced was what so many others have, that in setting a contract to be listened to he began to listen to himself.*

In order to listen, or be listened to, first establish a contract.

STAGE TWO: IDENTIFY THE ISSUE

More often than not when we listen to someone, we hear first of all what they want us to hear on the surface, as they wait subconsciously for us to pick up the cues so that we hear what they are really trying to tell us. The second thing we will hear is the message that is in our own head. The result is that we seldom really hear what someone else wants to say. An example of this is the first time that Claudette sat down to listen to Derek.

> *Claudette had already experienced what it was like to be listened to at a deep level during her Emotional Fitness training course. She now wanted to practice what she had discovered and when Derek asked her to listen to him, she readily agreed. Claudette, you might recall, was searching for inner peace in her life, and found it through her journey of listening to herself. Along the way, she encountered much confusion, often finding it difficult to separate her own*

thoughts and feelings from those people she listened to.

When Derek started to share his thoughts with her, telling her how negative and confused he was feeling about his life, Claudette believed that she knew exactly what he was talking about, and what he was experiencing. Claudette was delighted. Here was someone who was talking about something that she could really resonate with. She wasn't the only person who was confused! If she could just help Derek to understand that he was not alone in his confusion, perhaps he would feel better about it. As Claudette told Derek that she understood him, and that being confused was just an important phase, and that she felt the same way much of the time, she noticed that he was showing signs of discomfort, moving around in his chair, looking away from her, his face turning a deeper pink, his lips appearing to clamp themselves together.

Suddenly he exploded, his face turning a now brilliant red. "You're supposed to be listening to me," he shouted. "All you've done is to tell me how I'm supposed to feel. I'm telling you that I'm stuck. I just don't know how to get out of this feeling of being worthless. And you're not helping."

Claudette learned a great lesson in that moment, or rather in the moment a little later when she reflected on what had happened. She remembered that she had listened to Derek talk about a few things when he had started, and that she had focused on the words that were also her own issues. What Derek had really wanted to talk about was not what Claudette had wanted to hear. To put it another way, she had preferred to hear the things that she wanted to deal with herself. Now she knew what she could have done. She could have stayed with what Derek was expressing, not wandered off into her own thoughts and feelings. Had she really been with him, she would have heard Derek say that he felt down, that he felt stuck and that he felt worthless. She also would have heard him say that he wanted help, and that he became angry when he perceived that he failed to get the help he needed. She would also have noticed that when he did get angry, Derek became very clear about what he wanted, not the least confused.

Fortunately, for both Claudette and Derek, that's exactly what she was able to give back to Derek after he had his outburst.

When Derek heard Claudette say those things back to him, Derek became calm and contrite, apologizing for losing his temper, and then realized that his expression of anger was probably just what he needed. What happened, although not immediately, was that Derek discovered that when he really got to express

Assumptions are the death of communication.

himself in an energetic way (and anger was just one way), he began to feel less stuck, more able to seek help and more worthy of receiving it. What's more, Derek found that he could take far more control over his own life than he imagined, just by identifying what was really going on in him, with the help of someone who would listen well to him.

As for Claudette, she learned more about getting out of the way when listening to another person, and she learned that in order to hear what someone else is saying, she had to help them to identify what it was that they really wanted to share, which may not be the obvious or the first issue presented. Ironically, this helped Claudette with her own issues of confusion and finding peace of mind. She discovered that when she was able to hear what someone else wanted to say without mixing her own thoughts with theirs, she became clearer and more at peace with herself. The clearer she became at giving back to the other person just what they were saying, the less confused she became with how she felt.

The second stage in the process of Listening Power is to identify what it is that the other person wants to say. This is when we get to hear fully and when the other person hears him or herself fully, perhaps for the first time. It is a liberating experience. All we have to know is how to do it.

I find two golden rules more valuable than any other. They are simple to say, but may appear to be in conflict, which is why they are pretty hard to follow in practice. When you want to hear someone fully the two rules are to relax and to concentrate.

Relaxed concentration may not come easily unless you practice yoga, meditation or other similar processes. Inner Balancing, in the hands of a skilled practitioner will be carried out with relaxed concentration and is a joy to experience for both parties.

When preparing to hear someone else, first become aware of yourself, your state of mind, your body, your breathing, how you are feeling. Take a little time – it may only need a few seconds – to notice yourself and to breathe deeply. Then consciously let go of anything that you may be holding onto. This is easier said than done and is why we each need to continue on a process of our own self-understanding in order to give the best we can in listening to others. Once you become more aware of yourself you have a better chance of becoming more relaxed and letting go of whatever gives you tension. Noticing, for example, that you are feeling some anxiety about being able to hear someone as well as they want you to means that you are holding on to an egocentric expectation. This is a normal human response.

Being aware of that thought can allow you to dispel it by knowing that you will be the best you can anyway and that the other person will simply benefit from you being there. Now you have a better chance of getting out of the way and relaxing. Having relaxed you are now in a good place to concentrate on the other person.

Without the relaxation, concentrating means trying to remember everything that is said, all the non-verbal signals given out, all the techniques you have learned and at the same time trying to formulate the most helpful response you can make. This kind of concentration becomes mechanical, often obvious, usually sterile and almost always exhausting for both the listener and the talker. Relaxed concentration means being fully with the talker, gathering the essence of what is being presented and giving back this essence.

I recall one of the first counselling sessions I ever gave as a professional, after having studied and received my certification from the British Association of Counselling in the 1970s. A woman made an appointment to see me because, as she had said on the 'phone, "I'm having a lot of anxiety attacks." She came through the door and I was struck by her somewhat bizarre appearance, covered as she was almost from head to toe with a flowing black robe, a circle of black beads wound around her very blonde hair and extraordinarily long fingernails painted black. I asked her to tell me about her anxiety and she described what happened. It seemed that she had these 'attacks' in the late afternoons when she was at home. I asked her to say what happened at those times.

"It's when my son comes home from school," she said.

"Yes?"

"Well, we have a cup of tea and a chocolate bar. I love those."

She named a brand of a chocolate bar that had been one of my favourites as a child, although I hadn't had one for years.

"Then what?"

"Sometimes I have two bars." She looked at me. "To tell you the truth, I even have three most times. My son laughs at me. He just can't believe how I can eat that many and not be sick."

There appeared to be no other cause for her to become anxious at that or any other time, so I suggested that there may be a connection between her eating the chocolate and her anxiety attacks.

How you feel is what we get.

"Try giving them up for a week, the sugar content may be affecting you."
She agreed to do this, and said she would return the following week.
The following week she appeared, still wearing her unusual attire.

"Thank you doctor," she said, "I haven't had that anxiety since I stopped eating all that chocolate. Do you think I could try just one bar?"

"I'm not a doctor. Now that you know what causes your anxiety attack, you could see how the chocolate affects you. You can be in control of it."

I was delighted with myself, but my ego was deflated in about four seconds. I had not followed the psychodynamic counselling approach in which I had been trained, which would have meant working with her to help her discover the deeper nature of her feelings and behaviour. Instead, I had helped her make the obvious connection and suggested the simple remedy.

As she left, with her hand on the doorknob, she thanked me again, insisting on calling me doctor and said "by the way, do you believe it's important to be honest in everything, even if it might hurt someone you love?"

I often talk about the 'doorknob' or the 'by the way' syndrome. This was the first time I had consciously encountered it.

In the next five minutes I discovered that she was a lesbian and did not know how to tell her son. We arranged another counselling session. She did not come at the time we had fixed and I felt that I had failed her. I missed some of the important signals she was giving and had not allowed her to explore the underlying reason for her eating those chocolate bars with her son in the first place. I had not helped her to identify what she really sought counselling for. I had not heard her. Worse, my self-perceived cleverness got in the way of moving beyond the obvious, reinforced by her insistence on calling me 'doctor'.

She called the next day to say that she was sick and that she would like to make another appointment. I was saved. I heard her fully this time and after a while she found a way to talk with her son and deal with the feelings of guilt and remorse that she had been living with for years. It turned out that her son, twelve years old, already suspected what her sexual orientation was and was greatly relieved that she was now honest and open with him. It enabled him to talk more openly with her and to express his love and care for her in a way that felt better for both of them. Eating the chocolate bars with him had been a way for her to make a connection, to pluck up the courage to speak to him. The anxiety attacks may have been exacerbated by the excessive amount of chocolate, but the anxiety was deep within her in the first place. The clothes she wore were a way of her trying to say that she perceived herself as different from other people.

Most of what I have learned in counselling has come from my clients. Later, when I witnessed the listening skills of John Heimler, then developed the Listening Power process, I saw that the ability to hear what someone is saying comes when we help them to identify the underlying, often unstated, even unconscious issue that they want to explore. We can only help the change to come about if we have truly heard what the person desires to be changed.

In order to hear or be heard, identify what is being presented.

STAGE THREE: CLARIFY WHAT YOU HAVE HEARD

Having heard what someone has to share can often be an exhilarating experience for both the talker and the listener. "I've never told this to anyone", is a phrase I hear very often as the relief in their eyes and the relaxing of their bodies shows how much they have been holding onto an old experience or negative thought. It is one thing to hear something, quite another to understand what you have heard.

Let us for a moment return to Greg. It is some time since he was introduced to you, so here is a reminder. Greg was known for his wisdom and was highly regarded in his profession. He had experienced a difficult divorce that left him feeling very vulnerable.

When I met with Greg I knew of his reputation and felt a little intimidated that he was seeking support from me. Would I be up to the task, up to Greg's standards and expectations? We established a contract which included an agreement to have six weekly sessions and then review progress. Greg identified early in our sessions that his vulnerability now was a reflection of how he felt most of his life.

Here was someone with whom I could identify closely. I too, was regarded by many as being a wise leader and teacher. Yet, I also felt that vulnerability, often not feeling worthy of those labels. I too, had been through a divorce that left me with a greater sense of isolation and feeling unsafe, just the way I felt during much of my childhood and adolescence. It would have been easy for me to slip into the assumption that, because we appeared to have experienced similar circumstances, I understood exactly what Greg was going through.

Making assumptions is one of the most common causes for misunder-

The only coincidence is that you noticed it again.

standing between people. It happens because we are usually trying to help, trying to show that we do understand, trying to demonstrate empathy with the other person. The reverse is often the experience of the person we are listening to. Instead of feeling understood, he or she is likely to feel devalued and disregarded. "Yes, I know exactly what you mean. I know just how you're feeling", is a common response from people who want to show their empathy, and believe that what they have just heard is a mirror image of their own experience. When I hear that from someone I want to shout, "no, you don't know. How can you possibly know what my experience is, what my feelings are like? They are my feelings and I don't want you to jump in before I have had a chance to share them fully. Whether my feelings are ones of sadness or of joy, of pleasure or of pain, they are still my own unique ones. I will feel more able to share them with you when I believe that you want to get into my shoes and understand them from my perspective."

I'm glad that I resisted the temptation to tell Greg that I understood him, which would have been a wonderful excuse to start talking about my own experience. Instead, listening to my own voice and telling myself that if I needed to recount my own story again I could do so later on with someone else, I asked Greg to tell me more about his feeling of vulnerability.

His was nothing like mine. Mine was derived from the loss of my mother and other close family members when I was young. Greg's was out of the high expectations put on him by his parents. Mine was to do with the fear of abandonment in any relationship. His was the fear of failure as he came close to achieving his goals.

In asking questions and mirroring back to Greg what I heard, I began to understand more about Greg. As Greg answered my questions and received my feedback he became clearer about himself and his patterns.

The questions are not an interrogation, nor are they to develop an analysis of the person so that we can come to a conclusion about them. Inner Balancing is not an analytical approach. It is not one where we interpret what someone tells us in order to tell them who they are, what personality traits they have or what they have to do to change their behaviour. Inner Balancing is an approach that helps people to understand themselves more clearly.

The questions we ask are those that help to clarify what someone is presenting.

In this process of understanding we begin to hear and see the patterns emerging. The same or similar words and phrases are repeated. The tone of voice changes when certain issues are talked about or people mentioned.

The person's body movements shift. All these signals tell their own story as we attend to what we see and hear. Connections appear between an experience now and one that took place years ago or between incidents that show similar outcomes.

In helping someone towards greater and greater clarity we ask questions and mirror back what we are hearing. Here is an example of a fragment of conversation. S is the speaker; L is the listener.

S *I want to let go of my anger. I've found that it has got me into trouble and doesn't make me feel any better. I just don't know how to do it.*

L *Can you describe your anger to me?*

S *It kind of creeps up on me. I get this feeling that I'm being manipulated, then I know I'm going to give in. It feels like I'm being totally ignored; like I shouldn't have any opinions or that I'm not worthy enough to have them considered. Before I know it, I'm feeling so angry that I just want to lash out. I usually finish up shouting and storming out. Then I feel guilty.*

L *You've said a lot here. I'd like to explore some of what you have shared with me. You told me that you know you are going to give in when you feel you are being manipulated. Would you tell me more about that feeling?*

S *Yes, I did say that didn't I. (Pause). I think it's that I want a quiet life. (Pause). No, it's more than that. I can't take disharmony. Can't stand it when there is disagreement. So I give in even when I disagree inside myself, even when it's against me. Funny thing is, that's when I get angry. I don't want others to be angry with me, and then I get angry with myself.*

L *You get angry with yourself because you give in?*

S *Not exactly. I get angry with myself for making myself a victim of someone else's abuse. I suppose that's the same as giving in, but I'm beginning to realize what's happening here.*

L *What is happening?*

S *I got a lot of abuse from my brothers and sisters when I was small. I was the youngest and they teased me all the time and sometimes got me into bad trouble with my parents. What's happening now is that I see I'm trying to avoid any trouble like that. When I feel angry it's like I'm being a victim again.*

L *So, if I understand it, you are saying that when you get angry now, it feels like you are a child being victimized by your brothers and sisters, and that you learned to give in to try to avoid getting into trouble with your parents.*

When something hurts, you know you are alive.

S   *Yes, and I'm still doing that thirty years later and treating other people like*
     they're my family and I'm a kid. I don't have to do that do I?
L   *You mean you want to change that?*
S   *Absolutely.*

From this brief excerpt you can see that the desire to let go of anger has become a desire to change an old habit of learned behaviour that was necessary for a child to survive, but is no longer needed by the adult. Greater clarity leading to more of an understanding by the speaker will in turn lead to a higher level of awareness so that this person will notice the feelings of being made a victim and can change that perception. This is bound to lead to better relationships.

Notice something else as well. The listener is accepting what the speaker is saying, is taking it seriously and treating it with respect. In Eric Berne's terms, using his approach of Transactional Analysis, the listener is coming from an adult ego state. The response back from the speaker is in turn adult, since he or she is treated as being OK. Imagine another probably more usual, scenario in which the speaker having said – "I want to let go of my anger. I've found that it has got me into trouble and doesn't make me feel any better. I just don't know how to do it" – received the response, "well, why don't you try to button your lip a bit more? You get yourself into your own trouble." The response is from the parent and the predictable reaction would come from the child. There would be no understanding, no clarification, no trust and no chance of a resolution of the issue. Inner Balancing helps us to choose the adult mode as a listener, which is, in Inner Balancing terms, Emotional Fitness.

The search for understanding, for meaning, is really the central core of the process of Listening Power. The first stage is to establish a contract for listening, the second is to identify what the person really wants to talk about so that you properly hear them. The third is how to help the person to clarify what he or she is saying so that they and you understand its essential meaning. The significance of this can be considerable.

Once you understand the meaning of a part of your own experience, thoughts, feelings and actions, you are able to understand more about who you are. When you learn more about who you are and the meaning you derive from your life, you are closer to becoming who you really are. When you become closer to who you really are, you are able to become closer to others.

**In order to understand and to be understood,
clarify what is being presented.**

STAGE FOUR: SUMMARIZE WHAT YOU HAVE UNDERSTOOD

Each of the stages flows from the one before so that Listening Power, when carried out well, is a seamless process. While you are learning the process it may appear more stilted and mechanical at first. Remember that Listening Power has been developed not from theory, but from observation of what actually happens when great listening takes place.

The fourth stage has already begun. It is a matter only of putting it all together. The effect of summarizing the essence of what the person has presented to you or handing back that essence as a gift, is surprising. When, without making any interpretation, analysis or judgment of what you have listened to, heard and understood, you give that essence back, it is as though you are saying, "this is what I have understood and this is who I understand that you are." Did I say that the effect is surprising? For the person who receives your gift this is often amazing. This is the moment of acceptance. In Transactional Analysis terms it is saying, "you're OK." Carl Rogers used his gift of empathy to demonstrate understanding and acceptance. *Gestalt* therapy holds a metaphorical mirror up to the presenter as a way of developing self-acceptance. In Inner Balancing the summary is saying, "I accept who you are and I invite you to accept yourself as well."

The summary is the gathering together of all that you have heard and observed and making a succinct, clear digest of the essence. It is not a regurgitation of everything or a memory display. It is less than this, and much, much more than this. The essence is the core message that you have received from the individual.

An example of this was when I was meeting with Maureen. You might recall that Maureen expressed a fear of relationships, some dissatisfaction with her work and was intensely uncomfortable in groups. (I want to reiterate here that, since what people tell me in the context of counselling is entirely confidential, these examples are not real ones but a collection of the kinds of issues that have been presented by different people. If you think you recognize anyone from my examples, this is only because many share similar situations.)

Point a finger at someone and you'll see three fingers pointing back.

This was Maureen's story.

"I feel I'm in some kind of limbo. I have a good job, but it doesn't feel like I want to do this for the rest of my life. I stay at home most of the time when I'm not at work. I'm a single parent with a daughter of fifteen and a son of twelve. Their father left after our son was born. I don't have any other relationships and few friends. In fact most of the time I just want to be on my own. If it weren't for my work I'd probably never go out. I'm thirty-three now and it sometimes feels that my life is over. I realize that if I don't do something soon it's just going to get worse.

"I was brought up by foster parents when I was a child; then after the age of thirteen by my adoptive father after my adoptive mother died. He was a kind and loving man, but became more and more depressed and started drinking heavily. I came home from school one day – I was fifteen – to find a note on the kitchen table, saying he was sorry and that he loved me and he was sure that I'd be OK. He left a name and address of a woman in Vancouver. The police came later and told me that they had found his body in the river. I was totally devastated, didn't know what to do, although I wasn't going to let anyone take me into care. I took a bus to Vancouver and went to the address on the note. I knew it would be my real mother, and I was right. I'd never known who she was and didn't really care. All I knew was that she'd abandoned me when I was a baby. I didn't know anything about my real father and didn't care about that either. The father I had was always good enough for me.

"When I saw her, it was obvious to both of us from our likeness; or at least it dawned on her when I said I thought she was my mother. She went almost hysterical, then started smothering me with hugs. I felt as though she was trying to get rid of all her guilt or something. Anyway, after I told her what had happened, she said I should stay with her. I didn't feel much. I was still numb from my father's suicide.

"After the first few weeks my mother made it clear that I was an embarrassment for her. She had three young children, whom I really liked, and a new husband who obviously felt jealous of her first husband and now of another man who was my father, apparently someone he'd never known about. My mother never told me about him, except that he was someone she'd met at a party. I'm not sure she even knew who he was.

"I left after her husband got drunk and beat her. I was terrified that he'd kill me after I tried to protect the kids. I spent a time on the streets. Got involved with drugs, but before it went too far a social worker kind of adopted me. He helped

me a lot. After a couple of months I came back to the home in Calgary that had been left empty. I spent a long time sorting things out, with social workers and lawyers, and with redecorating the house. Fortunately there was some money and I was able to go back to school.

"I met Kenny when I was seventeen and we got married pretty soon after. I always knew it wasn't right, but we stuck together for more than twelve years. A few days after Michael was born I told Kenny I could manage without him. He breathed a sigh of relief and moved out. He's helped financially and sees the kids, but we're out of each other's lives.

"I keep thinking about how much I've felt on my own since the day my dad left that note, or maybe even before then. I felt alone when I was married most of the time. Is it always going to be like that?"

As Maureen spoke, interspersed with my questions for greater clarification, she clasped her hands together, often massaging them as though she were washing her hands. She kept her head down much of the time and her voice was low, especially when she talked about finding her father's suicide note. This was my summary to her:

"It seems Maureen, that you are telling me that your father's suicide has affected you very much; perhaps more than you have cared to admit. Your own mother abandoned you, once when you were a baby, and again as a teenage girl, and your adoptive mother died when you were thirteen. You feel that you have always been alone, and that although you manage very well on your own, you now feel that you are in limbo. You are wondering what else there is for you, and realize that you need to change something. It seems that you are saying that there is something you need to clear before you can move on."

Maureen looked up as if it appeared that a cloud had lifted from her, her hands became still and she seemed more relaxed than she had at any time up until then. She let out a deep breath, as though expelling something that she had been keeping deep inside her forever.

"Yes," she said, "I do have to clear something. I've never been able to talk about it. My parents were so nice and kind that they'd never say anything bad about my birth mother. When I was growing up I always wanted to know who she was and why she'd given me away. They just told me it had been hard for her and she hadn't wanted to, but I didn't believe it. Then when my dad killed him-

This swamp may not be much, but it's mine.

self everything came up again. Why did they have to go? Didn't anyone want to take care of me? You know, I'm feeling so angry."

Maureen cried for the first time; and cried for a full five minutes. Then, smiling through her tears, she said, "you don't know what a relief it is to be able to do that. I think there's a lot more, but I'm feeling more alive at this point than at almost any time in my life. I think I have a lot to do and I feel ready for it now."

In that moment Maureen began to accept herself. In her case this meant no longer being afraid of her own feelings, nor of being able to express them. She was indeed ready to move forward.

My summary may not be the same as yours. In a way, as long as you have offered what you have understood as a gift to the other person and have shown that you are making a genuine effort to reach the essence of what they have shared and you do this in a way that implies no judgment, you cannot get it wrong, because the person feels accepted.

Feeling accepted by someone who listens fully is the opening of a door for greater possibilities. Anyone who has a relatively low sense of self-esteem, a lack of self-confidence, who finds it hard to make relationships or displays a negative self-belief, will not normally feel accepted by others, since their behaviours will not come across as endearing to others. You do not need to get everything 'right' in terms of the summary you make, you simply have to give back the essence of what you have understood without criticism or interpretation.

This raises a question that regularly comes up; the distinction between acceptance and agreement. You do not need to agree with what someone says to accept him or her. You may, in fact, disagree completely with somebody's views. Does this mean that you cannot accept them as a person entitled to hold those views? This is an issue of ethics and morals. We each have our boundaries. I find it extremely hard to work with someone who holds and expresses overtly racist views, for example. The circumstance in which I will continue to work with such an individual is when I understand that those views do not reflect the person who is expressing them, but are there as a response to a sense of insecurity or hurt that the person wants to overcome. This is usually the case when someone has come for counselling. If the racist views continue I would terminate the work, since it becomes harder for me to accept that person and this would mean that the work would be fruitless and probably counter-productive. Such situations occur rarely; in fact I have encountered it only once in nearly thirty years.

One of the great tragedies of our society is the inability to distinguish between agreeing and accepting or between disagreeing and rejecting. Disagreements have been transformed into mistrust and then hatred between people, causing massacres, wars and the scourges of our time, 'ethnic cleansing' and terrorism.

Disagreements or misunderstandings between family members cause silence, feuds and great personal damage that may never be repaired, sometimes for generations. This poison in our culture is caught by children and youth in society who come to believe that anyone whose views, religion or mode of living differs from their own must, by definition be wrong, bad, untrustworthy or otherwise unacceptable. In such circumstances suicide bombers become heroes and September 11th becomes a date of infamy.

Imagine someone who has always experienced that when they express their innermost thoughts, feelings or views about anything, they get rejected as a person. Imagine that, perhaps for the first time, they feel themselves to be totally accepted by someone who has listened to, heard and understood them. It may take some time for them to believe and to trust this, but when they do they may indeed open that door to self-acceptance, and acceptance of others.

**In order to accept someone and what they say,
summarize the essence of what you have understood.**

STAGE FIVE: RESPOND BY HELPING THE PERSON TOWARDS THEIR OWN ACTION

In a way the whole process of Inner Balancing is a process of transformation, of change, and that indicates action of some kind. This is inevitable. Once you experience being listened to and hear and understand yourself more fully, transformation is already taking place. Nothing will be the same again. Is this the same as action? Almost, but not quite, for Inner Balancing is also about empowerment, and empowerment means the ability to become accountable for one's self, to make positive choices and to act on those choices in a way that is the most appropriate.

Action means in this context, the process of becoming empowered to do what is right for the person taking the action.

There are two forms of action here. The first is tangible, something that

Inner peace and outer chaos make fine partners.

can be seen or noticed externally. Examples may be applying for that job, calling a long-lost cousin, buying that house, finishing that project, taking dance lessons. The second kind of action is intangible, the sort of change that is internal. Examples here would be having a more positive self-image, the resolution of an old anger, a new understanding of a behaviour pattern. These latter actions are the deeper ones and will almost certainly lead to an outer, tangible action. A positive self-image will likely result in, say, the job application. The resolution of an old anger might well mean the phone call to the cousin. A new understanding of a pattern could result in the completion of a project.

I recall the most significant moment of change for me. It was a piece of intangible action that transformed my whole life. To call it a moment is not quite accurate, since I believe it took several days or weeks for me to absorb and understand what had happened, but looking back now it seems like a moment in time.

I had been sharing with John Heimler some of what had been going on for me. The theme was to do with working relationships I had and how I felt betrayed by some colleagues. I began to link this with my childhood experiences when my mother and grandmother, both of whom had cared for me, died within a year of each other before I was ten years old. This was after my great-grandfather, the most significant man in my life at that time, also died. This whole period of my life, pretty naturally, was traumatic and devastating. My father dealt with these three deaths by blocking off emotionally. He could not talk about them. All photographs of them disappeared. It was as if the three most important people in my life had never existed.

Love, not surprisingly, was out of my grasp. I had been loved, had experienced it completely and unconditionally, only to find it withdrawn completely. I lived the following thirty years of my life unable to fully commit myself to love or to trust anyone else completely. The exception to that was the love and trust I had for my two daughters, which has been constant. I married twice and loved both of my wives, but the love I felt was my unconscious longing to fill the deep void in my life, a void that could never be filled by anyone else. What woman, after all, could ever hope to come up to the love that I had received from my mother, the woman who would always be perfect in my eyes? What woman could hope to gain my trust that she would not abandon me or otherwise withdraw her love from me?

In my sessions with John Heimler I talked about some of these issues with growing insights into the patterns of behaviour I had been manifesting.

This was uncomfortable! Now I was speaking with him about the way I felt betrayed by my work colleagues. On previous occasions in the group work we had done together Heimler had talked about some of his own experiences in Auschwitz and the other concentration camps. On this occasion he gave me back the summary of what I shared with him, looked at me with his intense, yet playful eyes, and said to me, "I have asked you in the past what was your Auschwitz and you have not quite understood me. Do you have an answer to that yet?"

In that moment I understood. Here was a man who had not only survived the terrible experience of Auschwitz, he had overcome it and grown to transform it into his life's work, into his very purpose for living in an extraordinarily positive way. I understood then what my Auschwitz was and that I could escape from it and change it into something positive for myself. I thought that I had lost the love of my mother and my grandmother and great-grandfather. I had imprisoned myself in that belief. I had lived my life since the age of ten knowing only that I was unloved and that my childhood had been an unhappy one. The truth was that I had never lost that love. The truth was that those who had loved me and whom I had loved, lived constantly within me. The truth was that the love was always there for me as long as I accepted them and their love for me back in my life. I had, after all, experienced a very happy childhood. In that moment I changed my past experience. Now if anyone asks me I can say with complete honesty, "I used to have an unhappy childhood".

That was my action. It was a deep, inner, intangible action that would have far-reaching effects on my life. It helped me to learn to give and receive love fully without any fear or conditions. It enabled me to embark upon my 'real work'. It allowed me to take the risks that have extended me into areas that I would never have believed possible for me including writing (which means opening up my heart), moving to Canada (which means taking a leap into the unknown), developing Inner Balancing (which means allowing my creativity and self-belief to blossom) and setting up the Centre for Inner Balancing (which means stepping forward as a leader). So the initial, intangible action became a number of very tangible and practical steps that have changed my life and, into the bargain, the lives of many with whom I have come into contact.

When you are angry with your child, remember who that is.

One such person is Jim, whom you have met earlier on. In his case, the processes that Jim went through are not dissimilar to my own or to anybody who has chosen to make significant changes in his or her life.

In practicing the skills of Listening Power and other aspects of Inner Balancing Jim soon began to hear, understand and accept himself. The changes, in other words, his action, were the intangible ones at first. Jim began to drop the notions that he was a victim of his circumstances, that he was 'not good enough' and 'couldn't get things right'. Once Jim recognized what he had been doing and that he had been behaving in ways damaging to himself and others by holding onto those negative self-beliefs, he saw himself as someone who could make choices, accept responsibility for his situation and his relationships, and be accountable for his actions. He liberated himself from his self-imposed beliefs. He acknowledged his feelings as being worthy and himself as being worthy of respect instead of seeing feelings as being 'unmanly'. He became more emotionally fit.

The tangible results are still being seen. Jim is in the process of changing his career from one that does not suit him any more. He no longer feels that he has to be trapped into doing something that he despises because he has always done that work. He is developing a plan to make a new career out of who he is and what he knows he can do. I have already described the difference in his relationship with his wife, and this extends to his children, with whom he now has a far more positive and dynamic connection.

At no time in the process of change that Jim went through did he ask for, or was given, any advice. The purpose of Inner Balancing is to enable people to listen and to heed their own best advice in the belief that once we are really able to hear ourselves, we know what is the best for us. Since Jim, like most of the rest of us, usually heard the messages that other people had given him over the years, people such as his parents, his teachers, his first wife, he became unclear as to who he was and what he believed himself. This is not to say that we should not listen to our parents and teachers and others, rather that we have to learn to discern what is right for us. If the messages we receive tell us that we are unworthy and we get to believe that, we will probably act in an unworthy way or in a way that is untrue to us. It is one thing to take advice because we do not have the experience or the understanding, it is quite another to be dependent upon the advice of others because we have not learned to take heed of ourselves.

Jim, therefore, came to his own action in his own way because he heard himself and paid attention to what he heard.

The action stage is the fifth and final one in the Listening Power framework. If you have been able to listen to, hear, understand and accept the person who is talking to you, the last part is simple, or as simple as any of the other steps. It is as easy as asking something like, "what do you want to do?" But it may not be that simple, since everything is dependent on that word 'if' and also on the readiness of the person to move towards making any change.

The first part depends on the development of your own skills. The second part is not within your power, since you can never force someone to be ready. You can only do what is yours to do. The trap will always be to move into the advice-giving mode out of frustration. It is always easier to see what someone else should do than it is to see our own best action. Sometimes you will go through the whole process of Listening Power only to find that the person talking says at the end, "I have no idea what to do," while it is completely clear to you. "Of course", you say to yourself "that person should take that job, leave that relationship, start saying no, feel better about themselves, stop procrastinating, risk that new venture." Easy for you to say. Frustrating when they just won't see it!

Two things to think about. First, never underestimate the power of listening. It may well take days or weeks for someone to come to a realization. I have had people say to me that they made a change many months after a 'conversation' we'd had. What they meant was that they had not been ready at the time, but that they had retained the insight they had received until the right time had come for action for them.

The second thing to remember is that if you are feeling frustrated then the other person is almost certainly feeling the same way. Forcing your own ideas for action will only increase that frustration. If the person resists your ideas this frustration will be immediate. If they appear to agree in order to please you and then do not follow up, your frustration will only be delayed. The other possibility is that the person agrees and follows up, then becomes dependent upon you for continuing advice or blames you if it goes wrong. Not a win:win situation!

Patience is vital in Listening Power and no more so than in this stage. If you find no apparent movement at this point you need to understand that this is a part of the process of discovery. There is almost always a time lapse

A smile today could save somebody's life tomorrow.

between awareness, understanding, insights and action.

**To respond to someone and the essence of what they have
shared, help them towards their own action.**

THE LISTENING POWER FRAMEWORK

Putting the five stages of Listening Power together, the whole process, or the framework for listening, looks like this:

1. In order to **LISTEN**   Establish a **CONTRACT**
   or be listened to

2. In order to **HEAR** what   **IDENTIFY** what they want to say
   someone is saying

3. In order to **UNDERSTAND**   **CLARIFY** what is being presented
   what the person is saying

4. In order to **ACCEPT**   **SUMMARIZE** the essence of what you
   someone and what they say   have understood

5. In order to **RESPOND** to   help them towards their own
   the person   appropriate **ACTION**

The difficulty here is in getting beyond the technical elements of this framework and into the deeper sense of what is going on, so that it becomes a natural, human process that comes from a real desire to communicate closely. It will help to look at just what is happening and at the value of having a framework like this.

Listening Power is based on the belief that we each need in our life the opportunity to be listened to, heard, understood, accepted and responded to in order to develop as emotionally healthy beings, reaching our own unique capacity for manifesting ourselves. Another way of looking at it is, once we listen to, hear, understand and accept ourselves fully then we can take the action in our lives that is right for us.

Jim summed the whole thing up for himself when he looked back at how he had been and how he now felt.

"I spent most of my time listening to other people, or listening to the messages I got from them about how I was supposed to be. Instead of listening to my own inner voice about myself, I had bought into the message that I was not worthy enough to do what I really wanted to do. When I began to listen to myself, I heard that I

had within me a great wealth of talent, and that I could use what I had in whatever way I wanted. That was an incredible feeling! When I really understood that I didn't have to be a victim of my circumstances, and that what I had been doing for all these years was to keep myself trapped in the box I had been taught was all I deserved to have as my world, I started to free myself. It was, at last, like growing up. As I began to feel emotionally free and more like an adult, I began to accept myself as worthy of more, including what I had expected in my career and in my relationships. I no longer had to put myself down. And, as soon as I really accepted that fact, I began to behave differently. I began to take the action that changed the way I worked and the way I related to my wife and my children. Most of all, I changed the way I saw myself. I experience life very differently now, and others seem to see me in a different and much more positive light too."

If you have been practicing Listening Power in the context of an Emotional Fitness course you will have discovered a number of things. One of the things you will probably have found is that this whole process, while simple in itself, is not an easy one to go through in reality and that it seldom goes as clearly or as smoothly as may have been indicated from the examples in this book. Making it really simple and effective is a matter of practice. I have been using this framework for nearly twenty years, so it is second nature to me now. It doesn't have to take that long! I have witnessed people who have demonstrated such an aptitude to listening that they have mastered Listening Power within a few weeks.

Those key words again that describe the framework for Listening Power are:

LISTEN	CONTRACT
HEAR	IDENTIFY
UNDERSTAND	CLARIFY
ACCEPT	SUMMARIZE
RESPOND	ACTION

One of the other things you might have experienced is that the process does not flow through each of the stages in the way that Listening Power describes. This is quite normal, since most people don't experience their thoughts and feelings in a straight line!

When Donna and Paul came to their first counselling session with me, they told

The present is the gift.

me that they wanted to regain some of the close connection that they had felt in the first years of their relationship. They had been married for eight years and each said that they had felt more and more distancing between them recently. When I explored this with them, Paul said that this 'distancing' had been experienced by him as Donna 'always wanting my time and attention even when she knows that I have a whole lot of responsibility at work.' Paul's response to what he saw as Donna's demanding behaviour was to withdraw, getting silently angry and bitter over what he saw was a lack of appreciation for his contribution to the family's economic comfort.

Donna, on the other hand, described her experience of 'distancing' as an increasingly taciturn and unavailable Paul, who had turned his back on her and the family in search of greater financial and material reward and work satisfaction.

This seemed to be the basis for our work together, and we established a contract for a number of sessions.

When we met for their second meeting, Donna revealed her deep fear of abandonment, based on her childhood experiences. Her father, whom she had loved and respected deeply, had been killed in a work accident when she was ten years old. The family had lived on a reasonably high compensation and insurance payout from then on, but her mother had become withdrawn and depressed.

In the same session, Paul said that he always felt the pressure to earn a good income to support his family, and that although Donna had never said it, he believed that she wanted the security of a home without a heavy mortgage, and a good pension. As he listened to Donna and to himself, he realized that this was the message that he had inherited from hearing his mother and father talk about money when Paul was a child.

When I asked them whether they ever discussed this between them, they looked at each other and agreed that they had not. I asked them what they meant by the close connection they felt they had in the early years of their marriage. The response was that they had done lots of things together, had enjoyed good sex with each other, and had similar interests. They did not, it transpired, talk much about themselves or their feelings.

In the light of this session, I suggested that we change the contract. While it was still a relationship issue between them, it was also true that each needed to explore his or her own personal experiences and feelings first. I suggested, and they agreed, that I meet with each individually for a few sessions before meeting with them as a couple again.

So the contract was changed, and as I met with Donna and then Paul separately, each identified different issues of their own to deal with. This meant that there were a number of new things to understand. The Listening Power process went through several stages of making a new contract, identifying other core issues, reclarifying what those issues meant, summarizing and making new discoveries, and finally arriving at insights and action that allowed me to meet with them again as a couple. We were back to the original contract, with a very different understanding as to what 'close connection' and 'distancing' really meant to them.

The Emotional Fitness classes taught through the Centre for Inner Balancing always begin with Listening Power. In groups of three each person takes a turn to speak, to listen and to observe the process. A contract is set up between the three at first, so that there is an agreement about who will be the first to talk and to listen, and what the role of the observer will be. The listener and the talker establish their own contract. Quite often when this is new for the group they will underestimate the time that it takes for someone to talk when they are really being listened to. Many times I have known people to say, "fifteen minutes should be enough, I don't have much to talk about," only to discover that an hour has gone by. Because it is so rare for people to be heard in the way that Listening Power provides it allows them the possibility of discovering how much there is inside them waiting to come out. So an hour is usually the minimum time, plus the time it takes to discuss the process with the help of the observer afterwards.

The listener's job after the contract is established is to help the talker to identify what he or she wants to explore. Since, before the start of any Emotional Fitness course, each person has written up their own Personal Learning Contract with the help of an Emotional Fitness Instructor, what they will discuss in these first practice sessions will be something that they have already identified as being important to them. Feeding back to the talker what has been identified as the key issue to be talked about shows that the listener is ready to hear what is being said.

The listener will then demonstrate that he or she really wants to understand what the speaker is sharing by asking questions that help to clarify, rather than making assumptions and jumping to conclusions, making mini-

You are the greatest expert on your own life.

summaries and feeding back what the speaker has said, noticing and where appropriate commenting on apparent connections and showing an empathy with the speaker by mirroring back expressed feelings.

When it seems right (and this is always a matter of practice and experience, hence the experiential nature of our courses), the listener will make a summary of the essence of what the talker has shared, showing a complete acceptance of the person as well as helping the speaker to understand and accept him or herself.

Finally, the listener will invite the talker to consider any options and possible actions that present themselves from what they now understand.

I invite you to practice Listening Power with a trusted friend or mentor. Make very explicit what you want to do and be sure that the person is willing.

STORIES, SIGNALS AND MESSAGES

Imagine that you are going to listen to someone else. Consider how you will go about setting a contract with that person. Think who it might be, someone who is known to you. What will you offer when you listen, both in terms of the practical considerations such as time parameters, place and so on and the way in which you will listen, for example being non-judgmental and attentive? Think also about how you will ask what the other person might want from you, bearing in mind that, since this is likely a new concept, it may be difficult for him or her to think of anything at this stage.

You probably won't use the word 'contract' at any time. More acceptable (less threatening) words might be "let's agree what we want from this," or "I'd like to start by making sure that we both know what to expect."

Here is your chance to try out your prowess in setting up a contract to listen to someone else. Go to that person, say that you want to practice your skills in listening and want to start with an agreement between the two of you.

Meet with the person you have invited to talk to you. Set your contract. Remind him or her that you will just listen and that this means making sure that they feel heard by you, so you will say back what you have heard. Ask to be told if what you say back to them is not a real reflection of what he or she wants to talk about. When you are both ready ask the person to say whatever he or she wants to talk about with you.

You will need to be prepared for anything. The person may start with an 'extended weather report' or by revealing his or her most intimate secrets. The likelihood is that you will get something in between. The point is that your task is simply to hear what is being given to you. Resist any temptation to say or to show that you don't want to hear what is being said. Once you have listened for a few minutes and when it appears to you that it is appropriate to gently, but firmly intervene, say something like, "I'd like to see if I get what you are saying to me, please tell me if I've got this right or if there is something that I have missed." Then give a brief summary of what you have identified so far and ask for their's. Listen to the person's own summary and compare it with your own. If there are any substantial differences, remember that the one that the talker has presented is the one for you to accept.

Having identified what the person has to say and wants to share with you, your role now is to help him or her to clarify and therefore better understand what the real meaning is. Not just what the words mean. This is more than simply an analysis of the words, to reach some logical conclusion. This is beyond the technicality of language. We have developed language with all its richness and subtleties to express ourselves. Yet our words can seldom convey the inner message of who we are. We communicate with words about twenty percent of what we convey. The other eighty percent is communicated through the way we say things, through our facial expressions, hand movements and body postures. Your challenge is to help the other person to reach underneath the words, beyond the language into the realm of inner understanding. You have an opportunity here to help another person to discover a little more about what makes them tick, to arrive at a place of deeper recognition of the source of a particular feeling or pattern of behaviour, or to see themselves in a new and more positive light.

When you meet with your 'speaking partner' you may have all these things and more running around in your head. This will almost certainly make you tense and nervous, not the best condition to be in when you are trying to listen. Once you have absorbed some of the ideas you have been reading here, put them out of your mind, take a few minutes to relax and concentrate only on the person you are with. Remember the practice of relaxed concentration. Always become aware of yourself and make it a habit to breathe deeply, to listen to the noise going on in your head and the tension that you feel in your body. Then relax, letting things go physically, mentally and emotionally in preparation for really being able to listen.

Do not take notes while you are listening. Taking notes will not help you

Everything is simple. We just make it complicated.

and may detract from your ability to listen well. Trust yourself to recall the important things and trust your partner to help you if you don't. If the speaker wishes to write down some things, that can be encouraged, since it is for their own benefit and use. Once you have finished, set some time aside immediately afterwards to jot down a few notes yourself using the headings that are provided here. There is always more to understand and this is likely to be a huge learning curve.

What were the main issues presented to you by the speaker? Write down as much as you can recall of what he or she said. This is their 'story'.

What did you notice about the way the speaker was presenting things? Note down things like voice, choice of words, phrases that were repeated, how you personally experienced the speaker, body language, anything that you noticed. These are their 'signals'.

Putting together your responses to the first two questions, what do you see as the 'essence' of what the person was conveying to you? Try to write this down in as few words as possible, preferably in one sentence. This is their 'message'.

Write down whatever you can recall of what you did; the key questions you asked, the comments you made, the times you felt stuck and what you did, how you responded to what the other person said or did or asked.

Finally, write down your own feelings and assessment of how you did and what you have learned in the process. ♫◄▭

Here are those headings again:

1. Main issues presented (the story)
2. Signals I noticed
3. The essence (message I received)
4. My questions and responses
5. My feelings and personal assessment

Now, a little more about 'stories', 'signals' and 'messages'.

The most amazing stories are probably the ones that have never been written. Each single one of us has a story of our own, which are really many stories weaved into one, the common factor being who we are. This common factor or theme will always be present in each of our stories. Listen well enough and you will hear that theme. It is like hearing the music of a particular composer. Each piece is different, but to the trained ear the composer's identity is unmistakable. An author writes different novels, but the style will tell you who wrote them. An artist seldom paints the same picture twice, yet every painting has something that distinguishes it as the work of that artist.

When someone talks, even when the topic is the same as others are talking about, there is something that is unique in the way that person presents it. Since my way of expressing myself is mainly through the written and spoken word rather than through art, movement or music, I tend to hear people through their stories. If you are more visual you might see them painting a picture of themselves. Or you may see them as dancing through their life, or constructing their house, (or website!) or playing a game. I shall stick with the metaphor of stories.

Listen to the story you are being presented with. It may start with the weather or with a deep family secret or more likely with something in between the apparently superficial and the profound. Whatever it is, listen to the 'plot' and the 'sub-plots'. Ask yourself, "what is this person getting at?" Listen for the repetitive themes that come up. Pay attention to the mood of the story as it unfolds. Is there drama in it? Is it very complex or complicated to follow? Who is the central character? Is it autobiographical? (Every story is an autobiography underneath, but some are overtly intended to be). Is there humour in it and if so how is it used?

Stories are the stuff of life. Our real-life everyday stories are often as incredible as any science-fiction or romance or mystery novel. When someone is talking to you, whatever the topic, they are telling you something about themselves. In other words, they are telling you some of their story. Listen to it and you have the opportunity to help them to understand more of themselves if they desire to. When you relate back the main parts of their story to them it becomes more real to them. When you begin to help them to connect parts of the story to each other you are showing more of what they may have imagined was there.

The connections between parts of a story are what make it so fascinating and unique. Think of a mystery novel. If we manage to pull all the different strands together we can begin to make sense of it and discover the key to the mystery before the author tells us. I know of no mystery novel more absorbing than the mystery residing within each one of us.

The signals we emit are all part of the connections we can make. Watch and listen carefully for those signals. We pick them up all the time, yet we often ignore them because we are preoccupied with our own thoughts and

The most beautiful sound of all is the sound of someone listening.

feelings. Notice the expressions on people's faces, the way they move their hands. Now notice the connection between those signals and the words they are saying and how they say them.

Be aware of your own signals. You will need to make a conscious effort, since they are usually unconscious. Then connect the feelings you have with the signals you notice. For example, when you laugh as you say something, is this because you are feeling embarrassed or uncertain? Or is it just funny? When you notice that your hand has gone up in front of your mouth are you aware of something that you didn't want to say? Were you feeling some anxiety or a sense of insecurity? Or were you covering up a yawn? If so, were you feeling tired or bored, or were you feeling threatened by what was being said? Only you can begin to make any sense out of your own signals and your accompanying feelings or circumstances.

The same is true of the person you are listening to. Your job is not to try to interpret all the signals coming from someone else, only to notice them as a way to help you to reflect back what the person is presenting to you.

John Heimler was a master at noticing the signals. You will recall the description I gave of the first time I met with Heimler and a group of three other professional community workers and that he had listened to us and asked some questions. One of the first questions he asked was addressed to one of our group who sat in his chair slightly apart from the rest of us holding his hands clasped over his stomach. We had hardly begun when Heimler asked this man, "do you have a stomach ache?" "No," he replied, quickly dropping his hands and shifting in his seat uncomfortably. A little later Heimler said to him, "you seem to be uncomfortable." The man replied that yes, he felt uncomfortable with the ideas being developed. It was the first time he had admitted this. By the time we left it was clear to all of us that he was not going to be part of the team. It left us all with the clarity that the other three would continue and eventually create what became a highly successful community project. Had we attempted to continue with all four of us it is unlikely that we would ever have moved forward.

The connections between the parts of the story, helped by the signals that we observe, make up an overall message. Asking ourselves, "what is the message that this person is giving me?" can be a powerfully effective way of moving things forward. By noticing his discomfort, Heimler had provided an opportunity for that community worker to declare himself, freeing both him and us to move ahead. All the signals he was giving out had said to Heimler, "this man is feeling uncomfortable and does not want to be a part of this." All he had done was to ask one question, "do you have a stomach ache?" to eliminate the obvious and then to comment that he seemed uncomfortable. He did not make his own interpretation, he simply allowed the man to recognize and admit to what must have been going on for some time. We other three had noticed, but had ignored his discomfort. We assumed he was just being difficult! He had said nothing since he felt he had made a commitment and didn't know how to extricate himself.

The message of what someone presents is a part of what I call the essence of the individual. If our stories are us then we can discover the essence of the person through their stories, their themes and the signals. Once you approach an understanding of the essence of the person, once you begin to mirror back that essence, you are giving back the greatest gift that anyone can get and that is the gift of the authentic self.

This brings me to a valuable part of the process of clarifying what someone is telling you. Questions have an important role to play, as long as they are not interrogatory in nature, but intended to help the person make more sense of what they are saying. The process of mirroring what another says or presents is often more powerful than asking questions. So Heimler's comment "you seem to be uncomfortable," was a mirror of what he had seen. The option is there for the person to face the mirror and see its truth or to notice if there is a distortion in it, or to turn the mirror away. The response could have been, "not exactly uncomfortable, but I have a few questions I need to ask," or "no, I'm fine." This way the presenter is always in control.

The summary is probably the most empowering part of the Listening Power process. Anyone who can simply offer a clear, clean and concise summary that captures the essence of what somebody has shared is giving a great gift. The gift has two parts to it. The first part is one of meaning. You are helping the person to discover the meaning of their experience – of, if you like, a part of their life. The second part of the gift is one of acceptance. When I give back to someone the essence of what they have said it is the same as my telling them, "you are OK and what you have said is OK," except that I am telling them in a much more powerful way through my non-judgmental offering back to them of the core of what they have shared with me.

You cannot get this wrong. When you are genuinely trying to understand someone and you do this by giving them back the essence of what you have

It is more important to ask the question than to have the answer.

understood, you are giving something of great value. Even if you missed something or used words that have different meanings from those that the presenter used, what will happen is that the person will simply say so if it's important enough. Sometimes what happens is that when you give your summary the person will remember some other vital connection or realize that there is, after all, another underlying issue that only now becomes clear. Put your trust in the fact that the person presenting their 'story' to you is the person who is best able to make their own summary. What they may need and what you can offer them is a little help in untangling many of the threads and seeing the connections. Hearing your summary is the help that they might need. Once they hear it and then are able to make their own summary, they are well on the way to personal acceptance and accountability.

The action stage is an opportunity both to reflect back on where you have been and also to go forward. This fifth and last stage in the Listening Power process is in effect, the response to all that has gone on before.

The only way to enhance your skills and the art of listening is to keep practicing. Note that I am talking of the skills and the art. This is similar to the categories that go into the scoring of an ice skater competing in an Olympic event. Technical and artistic merit are equally valued and as we know artistic merit is a highly subjective judgment call. The highest valued skater and therefore the Gold Medalist, will score the most points in both those categories. It is insufficient to be technically brilliant without the artistry that makes the heart soar when you watch the performance. It is not enough to be artistically great without the technical ability to keep upright on the ice.

The equivalent of this in Listening Power is the technical competency to be able to understand and use the process without having to think too much about it, so that it becomes almost second nature. The artistic ability equivalent is creativity – some may call it the intuition – to know how to make connections and enable the other person to come to insights they already have within them, and help them reach a deeper understanding of their own personal choices and how they can make changes for the better in their life.

A word on intuition. What we call intuition is, I believe, no more than our picking up unconsciously the signals given out by another and our innate senses putting these signals together into a message. Listening Power helps us to bring the unconscious more into consciousness or to allow our 'intuitive powers' to be used more fully and effectively.

Take the time to practice Listening Power with someone you trust. Ideally this will be someone who is also using this book. In this way your contract can be a two-way one where you are both the listener and the presenter at different times. An even better way of going about this is to work with two other people, both of who are familiar with or learning about Inner Balancing. In this case the third person will act as an observer whose role is to feed back at the end of a session what he or she has noticed. Each of you will carry out each of the three roles of listener, presenter and observer. A great deal can be learned simply by being an observer of the process and discussing afterwards with the other two what you have seen and heard, in particular from the listener. Remember in your contract setting to include how the observer, if you have one, will carry out that role. ✐

If you do nothing other than become great at listening, you will discover how life becomes richer for you. When you practice Listening Power in conjunction with the other eight steps of Inner Balancing you will be amazed at just how rich it can become.

You know what's wrong with you? ...Nothing.

STEP 2: LEARNING FROM EXPERIENCE

I CAN DO THAT?

Experience is not what happens to you; it is what you do with what happens to you.

Aldous Huxley
(1894 – 1963)

Mostly we live our lives from day to day, from one experience to another. Life, we might say, is a series of events. Sometimes what we experience feels good, sometimes it doesn't. Occasionally we will recognize an experience as a recurring one and may ask the question, "why does that always seem to happen to me?"

Trevor asked that question a lot.

"Why," he wondered out loud on many occasions, "can I never seem to get going financially? I have some great ideas, and I have the training to do what I want, but it never works out. And often, especially when I rely on others to help me to get ahead, I finish up worse off than I was before." When he explored what this cycle of his was about, Trevor began to see that he had never learned from his experiences and constantly recreated the same patterns, albeit in different circumstances, so that he had not recognized that he kept doing the same thing. Essentially, what Trevor did was to come up with a business idea, create a brochure, find someone who had a similar idea and wanted to make it work, but who also had no previous success, put some money into the venture, come up with a plan, then do a minimal amount of marketing. Typically, few people appeared for the services offered and, after six or twelve months, Trevor's partner would back off, leaving Trevor stranded, financially poorer and little the wiser, ready for his next venture. Trevor was, if nothing else, an optimist.

What if Trevor could really learn from his experience? Would he continue to do the same thing until he was totally broke? Reading this it may seem obvious to you that Trevor had to change his behaviour if he really wanted to succeed. Why did he not develop a more workable plan and follow it through? How come he needed to rely on others who had no better experience than himself? All of us create repetitive patterns in our life that do not always work in our favour. They may appear obvious to other people, but we may be so close to them that we cannot grasp what we are doing or are so attached to them that it is hard to admit that they don't work.

Learning from our life experiences is part of the journey of liberating ourselves from the web of self-entrapment that we often weave for ourselves and part of becoming emotionally fit.

Trevor's experience of self-entrapment was to do with his career; Fay's was to do with her relationships.

> *Fay regularly bemoaned her fate. "Why do I attract these guys," she would wail. "They always seem wonderful at first; but they never commit to anything beyond dating. The moment I talk about marriage, or even living together permanently, they start to waver. Before I know it, they're gone. This is the fourth time it's happened to me; I don't think I can take any more. From now on, I'll keep away from any serious relationship with a man." Two weeks later, Fay would be talking about the new love in her life, knowing that "this is the guy", not noticing that she was doing exactly the same thing that she always did, hoping for a different outcome this time.*

In this chapter I am going to introduce you to Learning from Experience, Step 2 of the Inner Balancing process and the one that helps you to review and learn from your experiences, both your past and present ones, and to manage your own continued learning.

PORTFOLIO DEVELOPMENT

I first became involved in portfolio development when I was in England and invited in 1985 to head up a government project to investigate the use of portfolios in the training of youth and community leaders. I learned a great deal about how people can best gain from their own experience. Portfolio Development – or Learning from Experience – became an integral part of my own work and that of Inner Balancing.

One of the important lessons I learned while helping others to develop their portfolios was how astounded people were when they discovered the breadth of their experience, the depth of learning that they had from their experience and the way in which they had turned errors and weaknesses into valuable demonstrations of strengths. The reason for people being so astounded was that they had never recognized what they had done and what they now knew. Most learning had been an unconscious process with the result that they often believed that they had little knowledge, and focussed on what they still viewed as their weaknesses. The purpose of Learning from

Experience is to make the process of life a more conscious one and for people to see that they really do make progress as they move through it.

Like Listening Power, there are five stages in Learning from Experience largely because each stage is also about listening to the person with the experience. While it is possible to do this alone the process is greatly enhanced by having a good listener draw out key points and connections as you describe your experience.

The five stages of Learning from Experience are:

Experience. This is the **story** of what happened, what was done, what was seen, what was heard, what was made, what was written, what was said.

Learning. This is the **discovery** that what happened has some significance for doing or changing things in the future.

Demonstration. This is the evidence or **proof** that shows that what has been learned from past experience is put into practice in the present.

Learning needs. This is **ownership.** It's when you decide to take responsibility for what and how you continue to learn and develop.

Learning opportunities. This is the real marker for **growth** and the sign that positive change is taking place through the action you take.

Again, the five stages of the Learning from Experience portfolio are:

Experience:	**the story**
Learning:	**discovery**
Demonstration:	**proof**
Learning needs:	**ownership**
Learning opportunities:	**growth**

When you take the step of Learning from Experience you will be able to write at least part of your own story, make a discovery or two about yourself from your experience, find out how you can give yourself some proof of your own personal achievements, gain ownership of your continuing learning and become aware of your own continuing growth. How will this help to improve your relationships? The person prepared to learn from experiences is more attractive and certainly more interesting than the person who refuses to do so. Just try it and see.

Nostalgia ain't what it used to be.

$\mathcal{Q}$

When I run Emotional Fitness courses using and teaching Inner Balancing I always let people know that I welcome them on the journey, but that the course is really so that I may continue to learn and grow. This had not been my initial understanding. It became clear to me after the first couple of courses when I was challenged to 'sit in the hot seat', as someone remarked. By that they meant that they wanted me to talk about some of my own experiences using the Learning from Experience process.

On one occasion the experience I selected was 'the youth accommodation project' I had managed some fifteen years earlier. I had all but forgotten about it, and when I did recall it, viewed it as a wonderful time when I had spent a couple of summers leading a team of young volunteers in finding temporary accommodation for young visitors to London. In examining my experience I began to see the extraordinary range of skills that I had used and developed during that time.

Firstly, having been asked to head up a summer project for young volunteers from England and other countries in Europe, I had to come up with a theme. With a small group, I engaged in some brainstorming and minor research to discover a need that could realistically be filled with limited time and resources. The need was drawn from the news of the day – thousands of young tourists arriving in London during the summer period without sufficient cheap accommodation, sleeping on the streets.

My task was to find the volunteers, find means of accommodation for large numbers of short-stay youth and co-ordinate the project with virtually no funds. The project was a striking success. In the first year we provided beds and places to meet for around 300 young tourists every night for six weeks. In the second year we almost doubled this. By the third year there was no need for our project, because we had persuaded the London Tourist Board to set up a student bureau which, to my knowledge exists to this day and provides information and accommodation to young tourists.

Only when I reviewed what my experience had been and explored what I had learned did I see its significance for me. I had managed a major innovative project, demonstrated my creativity and abilities to negotiate and brought together a strong team of disparate volunteers, few of who knew each other before and most of who could work only for two of the six weeks.

In reflecting on what I learned I realized that I had seen it simply as an exciting and challenging time. I never before assessed what skills I demonstrated and failed to take full advantage of them. When I explored how I now use some of those skills I saw that while I utilized some, I had not become involved in other major projects because I did not see myself as having the necessary qualities. I denied my own abilities and with that some opportunities for personal and professional growth. When I changed that perception I began again to take on challenges that would extend me and at the same time be of benefit to others. I continue to do that today. It has certainly enhanced my network of relationships and the quality of the contacts I have with other people.

Learning from Experience is one way to stop, look back at some of our experiences and listen to ourselves in a way that will take us forward. It is a true learning cycle that moves from a simple (yet significant) experience to a new and different way of seeing that experience. By having a slightly altered perception and understanding of your own part in an experience you can change it. That is why the 'ownership' part is so important. Without the recognition that you are the only constant factor in all of your experiences, it is impossible to change the way you experience life. Do you choose to be a victim of circumstance, or in control?

Once Trevor accepted that he went through the same pattern and, if he wanted a different result, he had better change some of his own behaviour, he became successful. When Fay recognized that her relationships were not about 'those guys', but about her own inappropriate signals relative to what she really wanted, she was able to manifest the kind of relationship and life that she sought, but had never believed possible. After I understood what had been holding me back I wrote several books, set up a major conference on Fatherhood and applied what would otherwise have been hidden, or at least forgotten skills, to launch Emotional Fitness as a concept and a healthy lifelong practice.

As always, once you are listened to you are able to listen to yourself more clearly. By having someone listen to you as you develop your portfolio you have a powerful self-development tool that, as you practice it more and more will enable you to achieve that sense of Emotional Fitness.

YOUR INDEX OF EXPERIENCES

Before moving fully into Step 2 spend ten minutes compiling a list of your personal experiences using the five headings of **work, leisure, education, relationships, and life events**. You may have seen these experiences as

Beyond therapy – is growth.

positive or negative. Whatever you jot down will be right as long as it is something that has actually happened to you or that you have done or been involved in. Think about experiences that took place yesterday or years ago. Simply write down one or two words that will remind you of the event or circumstance. And be specific rather than very general. For example, under **Work** rather than 'seven years with the Smith Corporation', it would be 'getting promoted to area manager with the Smith Corporation', or 'negotiating a new deal for the sales team at Smith's'. In Leisure, instead of '13 years of deep-sea diving', jot down 'the time I met the great white shark'. For **Education,** not 'six years at St. Crispin's', but, 'being disciplined for missing class'. In **Relationships** don't just note 'married for 8 years'; be more specific with 'my wedding day' or 'feeling jealous when I saw those old photos'. And with **Life Events** rather than 'moving house eleven times', write down 'the sixth time we moved'.

Some of your experiences will be almost as old as you are, others may have happened a week or two ago. All that is important is that they were significant to you in some way. Imagining that you shouldn't write something down because it might be 'trivial' or wouldn't mean anything to someone else is simply one way of trivializing yourself. If it comes to mind it is almost certainly important as a potential area for your learning and growth.

Another thing to think about is this; you may view your experiences as positive or negative, and you may be biased in your recollections towards one or the other. Experiences themselves – the events in our lives – are neither positive nor negative, they are neutral. How we experience or respond to them is what makes them feel positive or negative. Since we are capable of feeling bad about a particular experience, we are also capable of feeling good about the same experience.

Let your mind roll over some of your own personal 'life stories' and see this Index of Experiences as chapter headings for the book of your life so far. Give yourself some quiet time to relax and make sure that you are in a place where you will not be disturbed for a little while. Use the headings as guidelines only; they are there as a reminder of the different facets of your life. If you are unsure where to put a particular experience it really doesn't matter. Many experiences will be relevant to two or more of the headings; you need to write it down only once. You may want to think in chronological order or do a mind-mapping exercise where each thought leads to another. There is no right or wrong way to do this and if you find yourself thinking so, note this in your own mind as something you might want to focus on as you continue along this step of Inner Balancing.

Each time you come back to your Index you will think of more experiences to add, and of course as you collect more experiences over the next days, weeks and months you can add them too.

When you are ready, take your ten minutes to write down as many of your experiences as you can recall using a word or a brief phrase that is sufficient to remind you what it is. The headings for your index of experiences are:

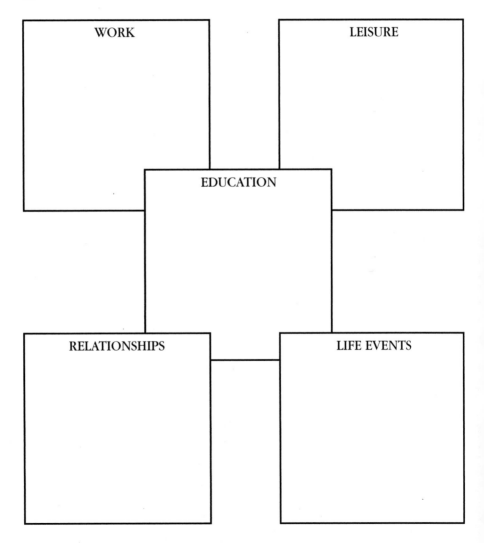

THE STORY

DESCRIPTION OF ONE EXPERIENCE

Select one experience from the lists you have just compiled. This can be from any of the areas.

1. Describe this experience to a mentor or coach.
2. Write down a summary of what you have said.

This is simply a description of the experience you had from your own perspective. You may have been five years old at the time or it might have been something that happened a couple of weeks ago. Try to make it as focused as you can so that you are describing just one event or experience that took place in a short time rather than a whole series or a longer experience that happened over a lengthy period. This is where your listener can be so helpful.

Remember to use the Listening Power process throughout these assignments. Make a contract, identify the issue (that is the experience you have chosen), clarify what the experience has meant to you and make a summary of the essence (this is what you write down). The action will be your next stage in the process.

When you are ready, and have shared your experience with your listener (or with yourself if there is nobody else taking part in this), write down your story. ✐◄▦

DISCOVERY

WHAT I HAVE LEARNED FROM THAT EXPERIENCE

Next, read back what you have written in your story and explore, preferably with the help of your mentor or listener, what you now understand that you have learned from the experience. When you are ready, write down what you have learned (discovered about yourself). ✐◄▦

PROOF

HOW I DEMONSTRATE MY ACHIEVEMENT

Discuss how you now use what you have learned from the experience just described. How can you demonstrate what you learned? Be creative and give examples to show what you know and can do and believe. ✐◄▦

OWNERSHIP

WHAT ELSE I NEED TO LEARN

Think about what else you need to learn from what you have said and summarize this for yourself to write in your portfolio. ✐◄▦

GROWTH

LEARNING OPPORTUNITIES I PLAN TO TAKE UP

Finally, look at how you want to learn and what opportunities you want to carve out for yourself. Do you prefer to read things, practice them, go on courses, ask somebody, or what? Give yourself a realistic time for you to carry out your plan. ✐◀▦

Now review your index of experiences. Ask yourself some questions about the experiences you have jotted down. Have you been specific, or very general? Have you put something in each of the categories? Are your experiences all in the distant past, or are they very recent? Are they things that you regard as positive or negative? Do you have at least four experiences noted in each of the categories? Notice any resistance that you felt while you were thinking of events in your life that prevented you from writing them down. Maybe those are the ones that can offer you the most learning. What stopped you from writing down some of those experiences? Listen to your own reasons, or excuses, or rationale. Notice how you are feeling as you hear the conversation going on inside yourself. ✐◀▦

Spend another couple of minutes adding anything else that comes to mind, and that on reflection, you want to add. Look over what you have written down. These are the potential headings, or chapter titles, of your own book so far; the experiences that have contributed to your life in some way. There is a story behind each one of them. As you get to explore them, you will discover that there is more to them than just the experience. Each can become an opportunity for learning, and developing a greater understanding of how you may make your experiences in the future better for you. ✐◀▦

DEVELOPING A PORTFOLIO OF EXPERIENCE

TREVOR'S STORY

> *As an example, here is what Trevor wrote in his portfolio. He selected the item, "Setting up my Internet business" from the section on work in his index of experiences. Trevor described this experience to his mentor, and then made this written summary. Note that this is different from journalling, because of the structure of the questions, and the fact that a listener, using Listening Power, helps the presenter to clarify and summarize the story.*

Without frustration we have no potential.

ONE EXPERIENCE IN MY LIFE

I had developed a new product that helps disabled people to open and handle things more easily. I wanted to market this through the Internet, so I spoke with a friend of mine who is good with this kind of technology. He said he could do it and wanted to go into partnership with me. After about six months plus a lot of money which I invested, we had a web site, but no real marketing plan. I had thought my friend was going to do this, while I continued to work on the product. In the end, the money ran out and my friend said that he didn't want to continue unless I was able to pay him. This kind of thing has happened before. My friend had lots of great ideas, but never seemed to put them into practice.

DISCOVERY

WHAT I HAVE LEARNED FROM THAT EXPERIENCE

This seems to be a pattern for me. I don't have the confidence to 'go it alone', and I rely on people whom I like and who have good ideas like me (but no money to back it up!) I realize that I have a great imagination and can create things and make them work, but I have this blind spot when it comes to organization and marketing.

I also don't make very good choices in the people I ask to help me. I don't check out what I really need.

PROOF

HOW I DEMONSTRATE MY ACHIEVEMENT

I have this product and a Web site. Both are excellent. I have less money than when I started. I guess I could see this as an achievement if I don't let it stop me in the future and if it helps me to do better next time. My friend is still my friend. I think that says a lot about me and I'm proud of myself for being loyal and supportive.

OWNERSHIP

WHAT ELSE I FEEL I NEED TO LEARN

I could learn how to do everything myself. That will mean getting the confidence to believe I can do the things that I'm not good at now, as well as having the desire to do them. Or I need to learn how to select others who will really support me.

Maybe that's the biggest thing: not just to be loyal and supportive to others, but to know that's what I seek as well, and to know how to ask for that.

GROWTH

LEARNING OPPORTUNITIES I PLAN TO TAKE UP

I'm going to find out about the marketing side of a business. There are courses that include this or I can read a book or two. I'm better with a course, so I shall see what's available.

I will also write down a list of what qualities I am seeking in finding a partner in any venture I want to undertake. Maybe I'll find a coach who can help me to do this.

TREVOR'S ACTION

Trevor did embark on a course, and while there he met another student who wanted to make marketing more central to his career and who loved it. At the same time, Trevor worked out his list of qualities for a partner. They included practical things, such as technical ability, marketing experience and proven sales success plus a preparedness to make a financial investment in any partnership arrangement. It became clear to Trevor that he was seeking qualities that would demonstrate loyalty and support, so would be looking for some evidence of that in a potential partner's history.

With the assistance of a third party (his coach), Trevor met with his fellow student, and satisfied himself that here was a person who fitted his newly perceived needs, and was also highly enthusiastic about Trevor's product. After a few meetings, they sealed their agreement. Trevor's product is now highly successful and he developed a whole range, while his partner handles all the marketing.

When Trevor goes back to his portfolio, he can use that new experience as another cycle of learning for himself, and others.

Select another experience in your index and repeat the process.
1. Describe the **story** to a mentor or coach, then write down a summary of what you have said.
2. Say what you have **discovered** from the experience and write this down.
3. Discuss the **proof** you now have for yourself that you now use what you have learned, and write this down, being as creative as you can.
4. With your mentor, think about your **ownership** of your experience and

Act as though you are the world's major power. Wisely.

what else you need to learn in relation to what you have said. Summarize this and write it down. 𝒪⊂▭

5.   Look at your own desired **growth** and what learning opportunities you want to carve out for yourself. 𝒪⊂▭

Do this for at least three experiences, and as many times as you want.

After that, consider what you require of yourself. You might see this in a number of ways. Do you want to develop your skills in a new area so that you can get different work? Do you want to improve your leadership abilities? Do you want to gain enhanced interpersonal skills? Do you want to improve specific relationships? Ask your mentor to help with this one. Note all the main things that you wish to achieve for yourself, then how you are already showing that you are achieving them. You might be surprised with what you find. 𝒪⊂▭

You will probably still have some areas where you are unable to prove to yourself that you are achieving what you want. This indicates only that you have (and hopefully recognize) a learning need. Indicate here what qualities you still require and show how you plan to learn them. Looking at the qualities you require of yourself is a way of taking ownership of your life. 𝒪⊂▭

Expand on how you are going to take your personal growth plan forward. Say what you intend to do, the results you seek for yourself, and how and when you will carry out your plan. 𝒪⊂▭

When you have completed a piece of your growth plan jot the results down. Don't omit anything that may not have been a part of your plan, but that you now recognize as a learning opportunity that you were able to use for yourself. Don't forget, either, the informal or unintended learning gains that you made as a result of new experiences. What you will realize now is that you are able to use any kind of experience as a learning process, and that this leads to new knowledge, skills and understanding. So note what new experiences you have had during your conscious journey in your learning plan and what new stories you are building up in your life. 𝒪⊂▭

Once Trevor started to learn from his failed business experiences, instead of feeling bad about them, he began to feel good about his ability to bounce back, and about his creative ideas. That helped him to concentrate on those strengths, and to acknowledge his weaknesses. Instead of finding partners who mirrored his strengths and weaknesses, he found someone who complemented them, someone who was a good organizer and marketer, although he didn't have Trevor's flair for ideas.

When Fay was able to look more clearly at how she fell into relationships that didn't work for her, she saw that she had seen herself as having had bad experiences, which set herself up to fail in the next one, because she had become so lacking in confidence and so controlling in what she wanted from the other person. Using her Portfolio helped Fay to see that her experiences also showed her that she retained the capacity to fall in love. This, in turn, allowed her to see what she really had to offer was that capacity, and the accompanying qualities that she brought to a relationship. It helped her to relax more into not having an expectation that one date would lead to marriage, and that when she herself simply enjoyed the relationship, things seemed to go much better.

For those of you who like something visual, here is a model that describes Learning from Experience.

Time will only run out when you do.

Marianne

 **STEP 3:** # LIFESCALE

ON THE OTHER HAND...

We all believe things about ourselves.

Sarah believed that she was physically unattractive, not very clever and not really capable of having a loving relationship. She thought that she could never have a job that would bring her much satisfaction and certainly that she would not accumulate much wealth from anything she did. Sarah knew that she had a happy streak inside her, but that this seldom had a chance to reveal itself, because it was hard to trust others not to let her down. She liked her gentleness and kindness with people, and especially with children (other people's children, since she had none of her own and of course felt it unlikely that she would have any). She loved animals too, and believed that she must have a good heart if she liked animals so much.

Sarah felt timid with other adults of her own age (she was in her late twenties) and reserved, even fearful, in the company of older people, or of those in some position of authority. She believed herself to be a coward, unable to speak up or say what was on her mind. In short, Sarah believed that she would never have a good job, a lasting, loving relationship, or feel confident about herself.

Three years later, Sarah is married with a small child, works from her home making and selling baby clothes to her widening circle of friends, has recently forged a partnership with an entrepreneur to market her goods, and feels that life, and she, have never been so wonderful. She has joined a network of business professionals, and makes presentations about her business on a regular basis. She knows that her husband loves her deeply, and she knows equally that he feels the love that she brings to him, to their baby, and to his two children who live with his first wife most of the time.

There are still times when Sarah feels this cannot be true; that she cannot really trust things to stay like this, that she does not deserve what has come her way; but those times are rare as she understands the remarkable progress she has made. How did Sarah transform her life, and her beliefs about herself?

It started one Monday morning at around eleven o'clock. Sarah's boss called her into his office and asked her about a report that she had just submitted on a project he had asked her to carry out. All that Sarah heard was that she had failed to do it properly, and that she was incompetent. (Later, Sarah admitted that her boss had said nothing of the sort; he simply wanted to understand some of the figures in the report.) Right there, in the office, Sarah had what she calls 'her breakdown'. She burst out crying uncontrollably, then fled the office, and finally went home and stayed there for three weeks. She saw her doctor, then a psychologist, and finally was persuaded by a friend to take an Emotional Fitness course.

Over the next few months, Sarah began to discover who she was, and that her beliefs about herself were based, not on her real self, but on the messages she had received from other people. She discovered that her parents had exerted a great deal of control over her. While they had always wanted 'the best for her', her father had always made it plain that he wanted her to take up the profession he had always followed successfully, and pressured her to do well academically, while her mother had constantly fussed over how Sarah looked, worrying about her putting on weight or her complexion. Sarah had struggled at school, seldom coming up to what she believed her father's expectations were, and, self-conscious about her looks, found herself disliking her hair, her face, her figure, as she grew into womanhood.

Sarah learned how she had passed on these feelings of academic under-achievement into her working life, turned her self-consciousness into timidity with her friends, her fear of her father's disfavour into fear of anyone older or in authority, and the conditional love she felt she had received into a lack of trust of anyone with whom she came into close contact. She also learned how she had turned all of these feelings into her belief system about herself and that her beliefs had in turn affected all of her experiences.

Eventually Sarah learned how to transform her beliefs, then her feelings about herself, and finally her experiences, by listening to herself through sharing her thoughts with others and receiving their feedback.

The Listening Power process that she used allowed Sarah to understand and accept who she really was and to take the action that would lead to her transformation. But there is more to Inner Balancing than listening, important

though it is.

The transforming of negative thoughts, feelings and actions into positive ones is one of the most powerful and liberating processes that we can experience. In the concentration camps of Nazi Germany, Eugene Heimler discovered that he could survive in a totally negative environment by recalling his earlier happy life and by being determined to make a positive contribution in the future. The result was that he made several attempts to escape, allowing himself to retain his sense of who he was. Fortunately for him and for us he neither escaped (when he would surely have been caught and shot) nor were his attempts discovered.

I transformed my own experience of an unhappy childhood in which my mother and other close family members died before I was ten into one where I rediscovered the love that I had received from those family members. I found that not only can one transform the present; it is also possible to transform the past. How we view the future has a strong bearing on how we live in the present. The pessimist sees the future in a negative light, which means that he or she experiences the present negatively. Time has nothing to do with our progress or our development in emotional terms. Past, present and future are all one, since it is our own thoughts and feelings that make time a continuum. Once I changed my perception of my childhood and transformed it into a happy one, my future looked much brighter and my present was, still is and always will be fulfilled and joyful in spite of what may be going on around me. That's not to say I always feel great, but I know that my life is, in essence, far more full of satisfaction than it is of frustration.

Sarah had experienced a life more of frustration than satisfaction until she faced those frustrations and began to understand and then transform them. She was helped by using the Lifescale, your third step to Emotional Fitness. This is the process that gives Inner Balancing its name. The Lifescale helps us to measure and understand the emotional balance we feel in our lives, the inner balance between our satisfactions - our positive emotional energy and our frustrations - our negative emotional energy.

To love your enemy, understand yourself.

The Lifescale looks like this:

THE LIFESCALE

© Warren Redman 1994

NAME   DATE

Score each question on a scale 0 - 20

1. How much PLEASURE do I get from life? ....☐

2. How much PAIN do I feel I have? ....☐

3. How much PURPOSE do I have in my life? ....☐

4. How much do PROBLEMS weigh me down? ....☐

5. How much do I feel I'm in the right PLACE? ....☐

6. How much PREJUDICE do I feel against me? ....☐

7. How much POWER do I feel I have? ....☐

8. How much POVERTY do I feel I have? ....☐

9. How much PEACE of mind do I feel? ....☐

10. How much PRESSURE do I feel is on me? ....☐

TOTAL SCORES (add each column) ....☐ ..☐

Jot down your own scores.

Here is Sarah's Lifescale, the first time she did one.

THE LIFESCALE

© Warren Redman 1994

NAME **Sarah B.**   DATE **Sept 26, '99**

Score each question on a scale 0 - 20

1. How much PLEASURE do I get from life? **10**

2. How much PAIN do I feel I have? **12**

3. How much PURPOSE do I have in my life? **6**

4. How much do PROBLEMS weigh me down? **10**

5. How much do I feel I'm in the right PLACE? **5**

6. How much PREJUDICE do I feel against me? **8**

7. How much POWER do I feel I have? **5**

8. How much POVERTY do I feel I have? **8**

9. How much PEACE of mind do I feel? **8**

10. How much PRESSURE do I feel is on me? **12**

TOTAL SCORES (add each column) .... **34** ... **50**

Life doesn't come with a tool-kit. Yet we still have to make it.

These are Sarah's answers to the question, "what does your score mean to you?"

I gave 10 for how much pleasure I feel I have in my life. I think this mostly means the pleasure I get from my hobby, which is sewing – mainly making clothes, and from my dog, who is such a joy to me. I also love the time I spend with my sister's kids. I baby-sit for them when I can, and I get on with them really well.

I have 12 for how much pain I feel I have. I think that's mostly because I don't have children of my own. It gets me down sometimes, more than I even admit to myself. I never let anyone else know that, because it makes it worse, when they look at me like they feel sorry for me; or when they try to cheer me up and tell me I can do something about it if I want. I also feel quite a bit of pain because I don't have a relationship. I don't much like my job, and I feel stuck in it, so that's painful too.

My score for purpose is 6, and that sums up what I've just said about pleasure and pain. I don't see what I have to offer, with no family of my own and no direction in my work. I don't want to live through other people, and I don't know how to have what I want for myself.

Problems are a 10, which means that I think about them a lot. I guess I think about them more than do anything about them. Although, if they're only 10, I must be able to do something, otherwise I'd have put 20. I think I may be seeing more problems than there really are. I think the 10 means that I can't seem to say, or to have what I want, and that's mostly about how I feel about myself. So, I see that I'm the problem!

I found place quite a hard one. I gave it 5, and I think that's because I'm not where I want to be in my life. Where I live is OK. But I'd like to live with somebody – I mean my special somebody. And I'd like to have a job I really loved and felt I could do well. And I want children of my own. So 5 means I don't have any of those. But I do have a nice home, and I like the town and the neighbourhood, so that's my 5.

This was interesting. At first I couldn't think of any prejudice against me, but then I scored it 8. I realize that I feel people don't think much of me. My father wants me to be somebody else. He says he loves me, but I don't get that I'm OK for him. Even my mom constantly tells me that I should lose weight, or change my hair or something. So then, I turn against myself. Lots of times I say to myself, I wish I were more…something or other. So I even have some prejudice against myself. I'd just like to be me, and be fine with that.

I feel quite powerless. I gave 5 for power, and that only seems to be the thought that I do have my own job and place to live, and I choose lots of things I want to do in my leisure time. It feels low because I don't seem to have the power to change what I don't have in my life.

On one level I wanted to give 0 for poverty, because I have more than most people in the world. I have a home and a car and stuff. As long as I'm careful, and I keep my job, I have enough to live on. But I gave 8 for the reasons I've talked about, the things I don't have in my life.

Sometimes I feel quite peaceful, especially when I'm walking my dog, or doing some sewing. I gave 8 because it's not enough in my life.

Pressure is 12. I feel a lot is on me from others, mostly my parents. Also from me, but I'm not sure whether that's what I have got from my parents or if its my own message to myself. A bit of both. Anyway, it's more pressure than I need sometimes. It makes me want to hide away.

These answers given by Sarah when she first came on an Emotional Fitness course helped her to begin to carve out a different view of herself and how she could find more of what she wanted in her life.

When she made summaries of her satisfactions (the sum of her scores for **PLEASURE, PURPOSE, PLACE, POWER** and **PEACE**) and frustrations (**PAIN, PROBLEMS, PREJUDICE, POVERTY** and **PRESSURE**), things became even clearer to her. Here is what she said.

My total score for satisfactions is 34, which means I enjoy my sewing, my dog and children, and I like where I live. I am independent and I like that. I hadn't thought of that before. And I feel I'm really good with children. In fact I'm good with the things I like doing. I'm great with animals too, and I've made some clothes people think are excellent.

My total frustration score is 50. That means I'm a lot more frustrated than satisfied! Mostly, that's about not having my own family – a relationship with a special man and children of my own. I seem to put problems in my own way because I can't say what I want, or don't even know it a lot of the time. I just dwell on what I don't want, or that I'm not good enough to deserve what I want. That's what it is – I don't believe I deserve to have what I want.

Sarah looked back over her answers and came to these conclusions with little prompting from her listener.

To be the best you can, just be yourself.

My Lifescale means that I have hidden from myself the things that I'm good at, and let other people dictate how I see myself. I don't have the things I want in my life because I don't let myself have them, and that's because I don't think I am good enough, and that I don't deserve them.

What I need to do is learn to believe in myself. I have to stop listening to the messages in my head that say "Sarah, you can't have that," or "you're not good enough for that," and learn to say, "you can have what you want, because you are good and you deserve it."

The support I need for this is for people on this course to keep listening to me, and to remind me when I put myself down, or just see the negative. I can also ask others, like my sister, and my mom to do the same. I'd love my dad to do that, but I don't think he will be able to. But I've never asked him, so that will be another action for me. Come to think of it, if – when I can do that, and not concern myself with his response, it will be wonderful.

You can try the Lifescale out for yourself. Bear in mind it is always better to have someone else skilled in, or at least practicing Listening Power to help you.

There are ten main stops along the way in the personal journey of the Lifescale plus some 'refreshment breaks'.

Each of the ten stops introduces you to a concept that you will make personal to you. Each asks you a question. For each question give a score of between 0 and 20. Your answer will always be right, because only you can answer it in your way.

PLEASURE

Travel first of all into the areas of your life where you experience and feel pleasure. This is your own personal journey, so you will have to define pleasure for yourself.

You may get pleasure from loving relationships with partners, children or other family members, from friendships, from the contact you have with people in your leisure or work activities. You could have pleasure from animals, from hobbies, from the environment you live in, from the things you have. You might feel pleasure simply in living, although you might not be able to define what it is that gives you pleasure more precisely than that at this stage.

Pleasure might be seen through your achievements, through your fantasies, through your hopes, through your beliefs.

Whatever gives you pleasure is not only personal to you, it is whatever is going on with you at this time of your life. In other words, what gave you pleasure ten years or two years or even two months ago, won't necessarily be what gives you pleasure now.

Only you can know what your score for pleasure means. Even if you have exactly the same score as somebody else your meaning will be different. You are unique. You won't find the meaning of your scores written in this book. That's your journey. Take your time over this. If it's helpful for you to talk it over with someone else first and you are lucky enough to have that person to talk to, someone who will simply listen to you, then do that. If you want to talk it through to yourself or jot down some notes first, or speak into a tape recorder, or draw something that represents the things that give you pleasure, do that. In other words do whatever you feel comfortable with. Sometimes you may want to try something that is a challenge to you. For example, if you don't think you can draw maybe now's the time to try drawing your pleasure on a sheet of paper as part of your preparation.

When you're ready write down your summary. The question is:

What does my score for PLEASURE mean to me?

PAIN

Nobody likes pain. In fact there are theories that say we spend much of our time trying to avoid pain and the avoidance is what motivates us or prevents us from doing things.

Inner Balancing is not about theories of human behaviour, it is about an acceptance of who we are as individuals and how we can develop ourselves in the way that is right for us, so that we can become more emotionally fit within ourselves and in our relationships.

We all have pain at some time. The pain may be physical, emotional or mental. More often than not one kind of pain is connected with another. Physical pains like headaches, backaches or other muscle pain, ailments of the stomach, intestines, heart or other organs, and general, often 'mysterious' illnesses causing fatigue are closely related to emotional stresses in life. Mental illness and disturbance may also be caused by emotional distress, often with roots in some past trauma that has not been properly dealt with. Whatever the pain, it is real when it's in the present and it can easily prevent

If you feel out of step, maybe you've invented a new dance.

you from being as effective or as successful in your life as you would like. You can take a look at your own pain level right now by looking at this question. Maybe you have given a low score for pain: 2 or 3. Perhaps you have a high score or feel it's high: 11 or 12, or even 17 or 18.

Once again, only you can understand and appreciate what your score means. If you have given a high score, thinking too much about it might be painful in itself. Talking it over with an understanding listener can be an enormous help, or using those other creative ideas that you come up with. Drawing your pain can be a wonderful way of your being able to face and then understand, and eventually tackle it successfully.

There are two important things to recognize here. First, acknowledging your pain is healthier than suppressing it. Second, Inner Balancing is a process that helps you to look at both your positive and negative energies, each of which has an important part to play in the fulfillment of your potential development.

When you are ready summarize your own understanding of the score you have given and write down your answer to this question:

What does my score for PAIN mean to me?

PURPOSE

The third stop along your Lifescale journey will help you to explore the feelings you have about your own purpose. You might have a clear understanding about the purpose and meaning of life. Alternatively, like most of us you might have only a hazy notion or find that such questions leave you confused. The question about purpose is not a search for a universal truth. In this instance it is about your own feelings of your own purpose. Perhaps it has to do with what you have achieved or want to achieve in some practical way. Could it be to do with what you want to leave to posterity? Your purpose may be about relationships, about your own personal happiness, about your contribution, about your day-to-day dealings with people and your tasks.

The Lifescale question is one that asks you to consider the idea of purpose from your own point of view, and especially the one that comes from the way you feel about it. Even if you have no idea what your purpose is you will have a feeling about it. This shows the difference between thinking and feeling. Your journey is the discovery first of your own feelings and second the sense you can make of those feelings.

This third question for you is, like all the others, personal and in the present. You may feel you have a lot of purpose, or little, or somewhere in between. Your score will reflect that. Do not concern yourself that you don't know what it means yet, you are simply giving some value to your purpose. A great deal of purpose will give you a score towards the 20 mark, very little purpose will have you hovering nearer the 0 point. If you are not sure or you waver between feeling a lot of purpose and not much, you will probably give a score around the 10 region. If that is how you feel right now it has to be right.

Your score means something. What is it? The answers you give, like the score, must be right as long as you give proper attention to how you feel when you explore its meaning and as long as you recognize that the meaning is your own personal one, and not a general answer to a philosophical question.

You are into your journey far enough to know how you want to go about preparing yourself to make a summary. Don't forget that you can change the pattern of how you do it. The important thing is to reach the essence of your own understanding about yourself in relation, in this case, to your feeling about purpose. The discovery of that essence is the reason why I am asking you to write down a summary at each stage. Later on you will go on to reflect on all those summaries and begin to make overall sense of yourself.

You may already be aware of a pattern beginning to emerge. You might find yourself repeating some things. After all, everything is connected since all the feelings and all your experiences belong to you. You are the person holding it all together, trying to balance both your positive and negative energies. Your third question is:

What does my score for PURPOSE mean to me?

PROBLEMS

You will have noticed a couple of things by now. All the key words or questions along your journey begin with P. That is of no particular significance except that it makes for symmetry and might help you to remember them. (It worked for me!) The other thing is that they appear to be in pairs – pleasure and pain, purpose and now problems. That is significant. The first of each pair represents your positive energy, the things that cause you satisfaction. The second of the pair is your negative energy, made up of the things that

Everything we do is practice for the next time we do it.

bring frustration. How much or how little of each you have will help you to see how healthy your current emotional balance is, and where you may want to change the balance for yourself.

Problems are things, people, events, that get in the way of what we want to do. In other words they deflect us from our purpose. Often we construct the problems ourselves and use them as convenient excuses, or the problems are built up in our imagination and become emotional barriers to cross. It's not wrong to have such problems, they are part of our human experience.

Now that you have had a chance to travel along a little in your thoughts and hopefully your feelings on the problems section of your journey you will be ready for this fourth question. Rather than getting bogged down by looking at the possible range of big and little problems that might beset you, get into the feeling of them.

Think about how much problems weigh you down. A lot? Give a high score. Not much? Give a low one, on the 0 - 20 scale. Notice that the question is not about how many problems you have or have not got; it's about how much you feel they affect you personally, and weigh you down.

You may have many problems, but have given a low score because you don't feel weighed down by them. Some people thrive on problems (although they may deal with them by passing them on to other people!). You might not have a long list of problems, nevertheless a high score would show that you feel that they weigh heavily on you.

Your meaning for the score you have given will almost certainly say more about you, therefore, than they do about the actual problems themselves. That is true for all the key questions of course. This one highlights the point a little more.

So take a deep breath, think or talk it through, jot down some of your feelings about this. Listen to yourself as you go through this process, saying to yourself whatever you feel is really important. You may feel good or you may feel bad when you do this. What's important is that you are really listening to, understanding and accepting yourself.

When you are ready, gather your feelings together and put them into a summarized form to answer the question:

What does my score for PROBLEMS mean to me?

PLACE

Here's an interesting one, especially as you recall the different meanings you might put on what being in the right place can feel like. We all need to feel an attachment to something or some place. You'll know this if you have ever experienced homesickness.

Your place may mean any number of things to you. A physical location perhaps, a particular patch you call your own. It might be the general environment where you feel comfortable. Perhaps it's the feeling of belonging to a group of people that gives you your sense of place. Maybe it's the more difficult to define senses of place, like the place you feel you have achieved in your society or community, or organization or family. On the other side is the sense of feeling lost, in your relationships, in your self-esteem at home and at work, and within yourself, wherever you are physically.

Quite apart from the physical, mental and emotional aspects there is the spiritual one. Perhaps, for you, your spiritual place is the most important one. It will be linked to your other aspects of course, especially the emotional one. How much do you feel able to express your spiritual self in your life?

Note that the question, like all the others, refers to how you feel at this time in your life. Make a record of the date as you put your scores and summarize your meanings in the pages of your journal. Get close to your feelings about the question, don't try to analyze it. You need to make a gut response so that your score is a reflection of your real feeling even if you haven't given it much thought yet.

Relax before going on. Give yourself the time and attention you deserve. You don't have to take all, or even any of the ideas given in the last couple of pages about place into account. All you have to do is to make sense of your own meaning from the score you gave. You will feel good about the place you are in if you gave a high score, not so good if you gave a low one. Sometimes you may simply have an impression of what you meant when you put your score. That's why drawing is a helpful way of capturing your meaning. Have fun with getting to understand yourself and how you feel about these things. Be as creative and as playful as you like. You can even break the rules! (Are there any?)

This particular issue might mean that it is important for you to establish your own distinct place. If that's so, don't be surprised if you start making up

If you believe the sun rises, you must believe it revolves around us.

your own rules and using the ideas and questions in this journey to create something different. If you do, celebrate your difference, there is no place for guilt here, nor for rights and wrongs. Wherever you are now is your present place. You may be happy, unhappy or indifferent about it. But what does it all mean? Unravel it for yourself here. Your question is:

What does my score for PLACE mean to me? ◿◁▦

PREJUDICE

More injustice and hatred arise from prejudice than from any other cause. Some groups of people are the victims of prejudice. Others are seen to be members of the more powerful groups in society and therefore the likely perpetrators of prejudice. At some time, whatever and whoever we are, we may fall victim to prejudice, or, more likely, feel that we are prejudiced against. You may feel yourself seen as too old, too young, too tall, too fat. You might find you are dealt with on the basis of your gender, your accent, the colour of your skin, your disabilities, your religion, your beliefs, the way you dress, the place you live.

The issue here is how you experience prejudice, and in particular how much you feel you are prejudiced against. In other words, how much do you feel that people are against you? The reasons don't matter. There are never any good reasons for prejudice, since it is based on irrational fear and blind misconception. That does not make the victim of prejudice feel much better about it. Or does it?

Someone who felt highly prejudiced against three years ago simply because of who she was, now feels very little prejudice against her. She is still herself. The people who display prejudice still do so. But she has changed her self-perception and her perception of those people. She is no longer a victim.

If you gave a high score, you may want to take a little time to reflect on yourself and to make sure that you really do accept yourself fully. If you gave a low score, reflect on how you may show prejudice towards others, however unwittingly. Even if you put 0 for prejudice it means something. If you put 20 it means a whole lot more. You probably put a score somewhere in between. The point is that any score has a meaning and deserves attention, because you are giving yourself and your feelings attention.

Later, on the return journey (yes, you have a return ticket), you will be making sense of everything you will have recorded about yourself.

When you think about prejudice and how you feel it against you, remember that since it's about your feeling, it reflects as much on you and your own self-perception, and perception of others, as it does on those others. Remember also that Inner Balancing is about self-development more than it is about changing other people, especially if they are not ready for it. We are unlikely to change prejudice in other people, but we may be able to change the way we handle it and the way it affects us. We can only be responsible for our own emotional fitness.

Your question is:

What does my score for PREJUDICE mean to me? ✍

POWER

Power is, perhaps, the most emotive word of all, usually because people think of it as meaning the power that one person has over others. The irony is that those who have real personal power over themselves have no need to exert power over others.

You may feel powerful in some aspects of your life, less powerful in others. What matters to you? Maybe you feel you would like to be more powerful in the way you communicate your ideas. Perhaps you'd like to feel a better balance in your close relationships in terms of the power base each of you has. You might like more control over your life, or parts of it.

You might see power as being something totally within you, that you don't want to, or feel a need to express, or you may feel that power is something that emanates from you and means that you can influence others. Power may mean to you the ability to make choices and take decisions over your life and perhaps more widely than that.

Make it relate to you. Avoid making comparisons with apparently powerful people. You will realize that there is no point in comparing your perception and feelings of power with anyone else's. After all, the presidents of the USA and the World Bank may well put a pretty low score when they grasp what they cannot actually do. So your score is based on your own level of satisfaction with yourself.

Reminder: take a little time for this to sink in and to prepare yourself for the next part of this stage. It's probably time you treated yourself to something, at least some congratulations for setting out on this journey and for the

Your life task is the one only you can undertake.

progress you have made so far. You have, of course, the power to disregard anything that you read here about power and simply put your own interpretation of what your score for power means to you. Your only rule is for you to get as close to your own truth as you can. That's harder than it may seem, since we are fed so much of other people's beliefs and received wisdom of different concepts that it makes it difficult to arrive at our own true feelings about something as delicate as how much power we actually have. You may get messages from other people that you are a very powerful person or you may get exactly the opposite message.

Your score reflects your own feeling about yourself. Now you can go on and determine what you actually mean by that score without anybody else contradicting you. That's why it is essential if you are going to discuss this with someone else, for you to make it clear that you want that person simply to listen to you without intervening in your thoughts. That in itself is a very powerful thing for you to be able to do. The extent to which you can do it may give you an indication that how you have scored the question is in tune with who you actually are. Your question now is:

What does my score for POWER mean to me?

POVERTY

At first glance poverty seems to mean one main thing, just like a first glance at most of the other key words you have faced along your journey. It is the state of being poor, and that usually means not having much money or possessions. It may mean that to you. Equally, it may mean other things. As always your interpretation is the one that counts, and as always it is your feelings rather than the facts as you see them that count. You may have plenty of money in the bank, yet feel poor. You may have very little material wealth, yet feel rich. We all know of people who have immense wealth and have seemed unhappy, lacking close loving relationships so that they experience emotional poverty. Conversely, you may have come across people who have struggled to make ends meet but always appear able to help others out and ask for nothing else in life. They probably don't feel poor at all.

These are thoughts that you might want to take into account as you answer the question, "how much poverty do I feel in my life?" Bear in mind that this relates to now. Next month you might feel differently even although your circumstances may not have changed much. The Lifescale helps you to keep a tally on your own progress in that way without having to check your bank account to see how you are doing. If you feel a lot of poverty you will have a high score in the range of 0 - 20. If you don't feel much personal poverty, you will have a low score.

Reminder, the higher the score, the more need there is to treat yourself right now to a satisfying sense of relaxation. But don't miss out on it even if you have given a low score.

You can decide if your score means the money you have or have not got. Whatever your views about money there is little question of its importance in our everyday affairs and in the sense of wellbeing we may have. It is easy to ignore the significance of money when we have enough of it. It is also easy to get carried away by its significance to the extent that other things are diminished.

Your own sense of your poverty is the one that matters here. You may feel none at all or very little, and your low score will reflect that. If you have put a score of, say 15, you no doubt feel a lot of poverty right now. In that case you probably want to change that feeling. Before you can change things, however, you need to understand them. Saying, "well, I just need to have more money" is unlikely to be sufficient an understanding. If it were as simple as that you would almost certainly have the money or the sense of abundance in your life.

Whatever your score, think it through, talk it through if you can, with someone practicing Listening Power, jot down some ideas, make a drawing. The way you prepare is as much a part of your journey of Emotional Fitness as how you actually answer the question:

What does my score for POVERTY mean to me? $\mathcal{Q}$◀▬

PEACE

You are starting on the final two legs of your outward journey before returning. This question is about your inner peace, in other words your peace of mind.

There is little point in describing what might be meant by peace of mind, since it is so personal that only you can have any understanding of it in your terms. In that respect it is rather like asking one person to describe the feeling of love to someone else who may have a totally different experience of it, or like describing the colour green to somebody unable to see colour.

You will know what peace of mind is if you have ever experienced it.

Two wrongs don't make a right, they start a vicious cycle.

You might feel a lot of it all the time. You may have it occasionally. You might yearn for it, fantasizing about what it might actually be like. Perhaps you just grasp at it as it dances out of your reach, before you have to turn your mind to the hundred and one things that occupy your daily life.

Does it depend on things, events, people around you? Can you experience peace inside when there is turbulence outside? How much are you able to give yourself the time and attention, the love and the care, to shut out the noise and find peace?

The score you give is significant because its meaning is unique to you, not because it relates to anybody else's score. When you come to compare scores you will compare them with your own over time, not with another person's. Do you feel very peaceful inside? You will have a score nearer the 20 mark. If you have very little peace of mind at this time then your score is closer to the 0 end of the scale.

Here is an opportunity however much or little peace of mind you feel, to give yourself a moment to experience some by relaxing and letting things wash over you.

Your peace of mind comes from something. What does it mean that you have a lot or a little, or you are somewhere in between? There are two main sources for how much peace you feel. One is external, the other internal. You may well see that the two are inextricably connected for you. The external will be the other people around you, the things major and minor that annoy you. They might be to do with past events and experience. They may have to do with the burdens you currently feel you are carrying. The internal will be how you feel within yourself, quite regardless of what is going on out there. People who have achieved a state of peace within themselves despite the world's turmoil have almost certainly arrived at that point through much inner searching or have been born into the world, into this life, with an extraordinary state of grace.

You will be making connections soon to discover how your own peace of mind is as it is. In making sense of it on its own first, you will almost certainly see echoes from what you have been saying up to this point. For now, answer the question:

What does my score for PEACE mean to me?

PRESSURE

Your final key word and the one that partners peace is one that we all feel at some time. It may be clear by now that we need the things that symbolize our frustrations or negative energy. We just don't need too much of them!

Some people thrive on pressure, others get weighed down by it until they feel unable to function at all. For the former, pressure is something that is stimulating and motivating. For the latter, pressure becomes stress. The same amount of pressure can feel very different to different people. And the same amount of pressure can feel different to the same person at different times.

Like peace, the pressure you feel is probably strongly connected to the other questions that you have been facing along your journey, or rather, to the answers you have been giving. Like peace, you may see that your pressure comes from inside or outside you or both. You know that you cannot change the world or even other people, it is hard enough to change yourself. But you would not be alone in seeing pressure as externally imposed. All you need to do here is to approach the question for yourself as honestly and openly as you can.

It does not matter at this stage where you think the pressure is from or how you deal with it. It has little to do, either, with the actual amount and level of things you have to do, or the calls on your time, or the requests and expectations others place on you, although they will all add up to something. It is how you feel about those things, on the usual scale of 0 - 20.

Reminder: a great time to relax, especially if you gave the question a high score. The idea is not to deny the pressure you feel, but rather to prepare yourself to understand it in preparation for dealing with it and balancing out your life better.

You have probably been aware of a pattern or a theme in the responses you have given to the questions. The theme is like a fingerprint unique to you. The way you have dealt with the questions, the way you have travelled along this journey, is also unique to you, and a reflection of much of what you have been saying. For example, if you gave a high score for pressure, you will probably have felt pressured by the questions. If you gave a low score, you might have felt quite relaxed about them. This may help you in determining the meaning behind your score for pressure. Make sense of it in your

Synchronicity comes with consciousness.

terms. That means not just intellectually, but using your real sense of being pressurized, whether this is a great deal or very little. Whichever it is will have an affect on you. And on others.

If you feel very pressured others will catch that feeling and may be wary of approaching you. If you never feel any pressure others might think you are too casual to be depended upon. How others see you is a reflection as much of them as it is of you. Worth thinking about though, especially as you answer the question:

What does my score for PRESSURE mean to me? ◯◀▬

SATISFACTIONS

You have completed the outward part of your journey. Now you are starting the return trip. Here is a chance for you to revisit some of the territory that will be familiar to you, seeing it in a different, clearer light. The first part of the return journey will take you to your positive energy, which is where you gain your satisfactions in life. Those are the things that give you feelings of pleasure, purpose, place, power and peace.

The total score is the sum of your satisfactions in life at this time, out of a maximum of 100. It is neither too high, nor too low, but just how it is. If you feel it is too low or too high you may want to change it. For the time being try to accept it as a reflection of how you feel in terms of your satisfactions.

Your satisfaction score is the source of your positive energy. You have already made sense of each of the aspects making up your satisfaction. Now, at this first stage of your return journey, you can put all that together and begin to make sense of your total satisfaction in life, as it is at this time.

You can get to the meaning by looking back at the summaries you have made of each of the five satisfaction words. As you review what you have said, you will see connections that you may not have noticed before. Sometimes you may see contradictions. Life is full of those. Gradually, or maybe quite quickly, especially if you enlist the help of your listener, you will see the overall message you have written for yourself in terms of your satisfactions.

Do anything that helps you to put together that message. Notice the phrases that you have repeated, piece together any drawings you have sketched to see how they fit, listen to yourself on tape if you have that. Most important of all, return to the feelings you had when making your summaries so that you really understand and accept what you were getting at.

Then take a deep breath and write down the answer to the question, like putting together a portrait from the five aspects you have already drawn of yourself. It will be one side of your feelings, one half of your energy force. Your question is:

What does my total score for satisfactions mean?

FRUSTRATIONS

Your frustrations are the source of your negative energy, which in turn is the source of your potential, creative self. Negative does not mean bad. We need both positive and negative energy to function healthily and productively, although we need more positive than negative. Two opposing energy forces cancel each other out. Your creativity and motivation stem from your negative energy, so if you find that you have an equal amount of satisfaction and frustration you may experience the feeling of being stuck. Your frustration moves you on. Your satisfaction helps you to transform that frustration into the personal success you aspire to.

It may be harder to put together your frustrations than it is your satisfactions. Most of us don't like those negative feelings. That is why it is especially helpful for you to talk it through with someone else whom you can trust. The scenery on this part of your journey may be rougher, rockier, more barren, less attractive to you at first glance. But look more closely, and particularly if you have a companion who is able to point out parts of the terrain that you had not seen clearly, you will find some real beauty there.

Go back through all the summaries you made of the five areas of your frustration. Seek out the connections and the discrepancies. Discover the areas that feel especially difficult. Start to pull together the things that make sense and those that don't yet. Do not ignore words that seem repetitive, after all, they will often be the most significant.

Before you go any further prepare yourself again by doing something that you enjoy and will relax you. Take a break for a while, maybe only a few minutes, and pamper yourself. As part of this, try making yourself comfortable, closing your eyes and visualizing yourself in your favourite place, real or imagined. Soak up the atmosphere, enjoy the sounds, sights and feelings of your place for three minutes. Then answer your question:

What does my total score for frustrations mean?

Organize a fun-raising event each day.

LIFESCALE - THE QUESTION

You have been taking snapshots of yourself along your inner journey. Now you are developing them, seeing the picture emerge. A single photograph will give you just a glimpse of your journey, the complete album will provide you with an overview of it. In the same way, you are now in a position to have an overview of your Lifescale, that is to say, of your life as it is now.

Often the inspiration to take a new journey comes from looking at the photographs and having recollections of the last one. You may go back to the same place but do different things. You might go somewhere else. In either case there will be new photographs or different experiences and recollections. But first you have to put together your album. You have done most of the work already. Look at the meanings you gave to your total satisfaction and frustration scores. The next goal is to connect them up, extracting the essence of each of them, seeing where each has an influence on the other, where they complement or contradict each other.

When you look back at your overall summaries you may find that you already know much of what you have written. You might have gained some significant new insights into yourself. A third possibility is that you find that you still have questions or are confused about some aspects of what you have said. If you have no new insights at this stage then the journey has either been smooth or you have avoided some of the bumpy patches. Only you can know that. In any event, you will almost certainly have found a different way to understand and accept who you are. If you have gained new insights then those are the things that you can record as you note down the meaning of your Lifescale. If you still have questions or feel confused, recognize that your questions are valid and significant. Write down what they are, note your confusion. Do not expect to gain a complete picture of a new country on your first journey, you may have to return soon and explore a little more deeply.

Get ready as you move into the final stages of this journey by getting into your relaxed state, then go back through your recordings, ready to complete your response to the question:

What does my Lifescale mean?

ACTION

Now that you are approaching the end of this particular journey you proba-bly realize that something else has to happen. At the end of any journey there is always some more preparation: repacking your bags, checking to see you haven't missed anything, planning for the next stage that will take you on to your next destination, buying more tickets, getting the car parked, finding the door key, saying goodbye, saying hello, getting back to the everyday duties you left behind. But you may carry out your everyday duties differently or you may decide to change things more radically. Occasionally, people decide to go and settle in the country they just visited.

The action stage is the one where you are ready to change something. You may have started this journey knowing what you wanted to change and this has reinforced your feelings. You may have seen something entirely new about yourself that helps you to take a decision. Action, changes, choices, decisions can be big, or they can be tiny. They can be outward expressions of what you want, or they can be internal differences in the way you see things, or feel about them or yourself. You can also choose to change nothing.

Go back to your overall statement about the meaning of your Lifescale. The answers to your questions lie there. If you have been true to yourself, and answered all the questions as you really feel them to be, the action will be clear to you. Don't try too hard. Do not force anything that is not there or that you really don't want. That will mean you are not ready to take that par-ticular step, or it won't fit in with what you have been expressing. The key, as always, is to feel what is going on and to relax enough to allow your feel-ings to be translated into your responses.

Know that your action will be the right one for you. It comes from your inner self with all the strength of your being. Other people may well judge your action. You need to be aware of that, and prepared to accept the impli-cations of it. No other person can judge you for being yourself and for being true to who you are. Your action could seem a tiny step to others, yet be very significant to you. Maybe nobody else will notice that you simply (yet it's seldom simple) decide to say 'no' more often to things you don't want to do, or 'yes' to things you like. Yet the consequences for you and others might be enormous.

Your action may look extraordinarily drastic to others who did not real-

Wherever you go, there you are.

ize that you have been building up to something bit by bit, and now you are ready for it. A big life change, especially when it affects others, is usually sudden only for those others. If you are ready for one, it will have been building up, maybe in your sub-conscience, over a period of time. Perhaps the impact of this journey will have enabled you to know and to act upon what you really have to do.

Write down your action, and the support you need to help you to take it.

JOURNALLING

If you have been through the stages of the Lifescale you will be clearer about the emotional balance in your life and will have some greater insights into how, should you wish to, you may improve that balance or your Emotional Fitness. If you have chosen not to work, or play, your way through the Lifescale and only to read what is here, I hope that at least you have some sense of the possibilities and will want to take it further.

One way is to do some free-flowing journalling after which you may feel ready to return and go through your Lifescale again, or for the first time.

If you are familiar with journalling you will probably find no difficulty in writing down whatever came to your mind. If, like most people, you have never or seldom journalled you might like to take a peek into a page of what I would put into my own journal from today.

Friday, July 20th.

This morning I gave Nicole a drive downtown, since she is working there this week and I was going on to a meeting with the Board of the Men's Conference Association. Our connection on a morning like this seems so brief and I found myself already looking forward to our Friday evening regular 'date'. I referred to this in the car as we drove, aware of her preoccupation with making sure that she had everything she needed for the day. Her response was positive and warm. I recognize how much this means to me. Does this mean that I depend on her response for how I feel? Does it matter if I do? Yes, to some extent, and no I don't think so. I love her, and the fact that I feel good around her doesn't take away from the fact that I also, in a different way, feel good most of the time anyway. There is a quality of my feeling good with her that is in a mysterious way, quite different from my feeling good at other times. I don't feel dependent upon her moods, but I know I am affected by them, sometimes with a degree of discomfort that I would rather be without. I put it down to love. Is this the same way I felt when I was small and around my mother? When she died I know I felt abjectly unhappy and lost. Is that how it would be now? I don't think so. If Nicole were to die, or just leave, I would not lose the love I have for her, nor feel that she had abandoned me. What I would miss would be this special quality of the feeling that I have when she is with me. I wonder why I am now thinking this way. How come my thoughts almost always return to this theme of love and death? Why not, given my experience? Even after fifty years? Yes! It will always be so for me. Yet it does-n't feel negative at all. It has been a central part of my life and I have learned to turn it into a really positive one. It has made my life come alive. Now I am begin-ning to understand what this special feeling is that I have when I am with Nicole, with the one I love so much. I recall how I felt in my previous relationships – it was more a feeling of desperation. Now it is like being in a warm, "at home", peaceful and, (what's the word?) um, um..., like being absolutely in the right place – even when I feel frustrated that things aren't going smoothly or quietly. At one? Free? Maybe there isn't a word. I just know that it doesn't matter whatever happens to me, or the world or anyone else; nothing can ever take that sense of bliss (maybe that's the word) from me.

Quite apart from writing current, free-flowing thoughts into a journal, this would be a good point at which to review how you are progressing with your own personal Emotional Fitness learning contract. Take a look at what you wrote. Make a note of how you feel you are doing and any changes you want to make at this stage.

The best time for what's important is now.

Before leaving the Lifescale, you may like to see how Sarah completed hers less than a year after having done her first one.

THE LIFESCALE

© Warren Redman 1994

NAME **Sarah B.**   DATE **July 26, '00**

Score each question on a scale 0 - 20

1. How much PLEASURE do I get from life? 12

2. How much PAIN do I feel I have? 6

3. How much PURPOSE do I have in my life? 13

4. How much do PROBLEMS weigh me down? 5

5. How much do I feel I'm in the right PLACE? 14

6. How much PREJUDICE do I feel against me? 4

7. How much POWER do I feel I have? 16

8. How much POVERTY do I feel I have? 10

9. How much PEACE of mind do I feel? 15

10. How much PRESSURE do I feel is on me? 8

TOTAL SCORES (add each column) 70 33

At this point in her life, Sarah had decided to turn her love for sewing into some-thing she could make into a small business, while still retaining her current job. She had become far more self-confident, and had started to date a man whom she had known for a while but had avoided in the past because she had not thought he would be interested in her. He was divorced, with two young children, and, it transpired, he had been reluctant to become involved with Sarah because he had felt it unfair to bring two children into a new relationship. Sarah was delighted to connect with his children, who spent alternate weekends with their father.

This Lifescale of Sarah's reflected the change that was going on for her. While she still had not clearly established a committed relationship or child of her own, she now felt the possibilities. While she still had the same job, she was seeing a different direction for herself. Most of the changes were internal, to do with Sarah's Emotional Fitness.

She had done enough to manifest what later took place. She married her 'special man', she had a baby, and she gave up a job she didn't enjoy for a career that she loved.

Sometimes I just sits and thinks. And sometimes I just sits.

STEP 4: TIME CAPSULE

HERE I GO – BACK TO THE FUTURE

You are a success when you have made friends with your past, are focused on the present, and are optimistic about your future.

Zig Ziglar

The past and the future are great places to visit, but you don't want to live there.

Tom Payne

Living in the present, in the now, is a challenge for most of us, yet a state of being that is sought by many. The Zen masters, other Eastern mystics and, more recently, the so called 'New Age' healers, philosophers and devotees (New Age is, of course, very ancient), have long understood the value of just being. The oft-used phrases of writers like Deepak Chopra and Wayne Dyer are that we are, after all, human beings, not human doings, and that we are spiritual beings having a human experience, not the other way around. Yet we are intensely preoccupied with doing, with our work, with the tasks we have to carry out, with the responsibilities and duties we have. Our description of ourselves begins, more often than not, with a description of what we do, as though that defines who we are. That is seldom the case. Since most people do things because they feel they have to ('I work to make a living so that I can do or have the things I want'; 'I walk the dog in the rain because it's my turn'), we mostly don't get to discover who we really are, or what we really want to do.

Being in the present, means…just being. It means loving the experience of the work I am doing right now, even if it seems a menial or, to others, a boring task. It means enjoying every raindrop that falls and the dog's muddy paws, even when I get up from a warm, comfortable sofa to do this. What distracts us from this enjoyment of life in the present is the thought of some other work I wish I were doing, like being a surf instructor on Bondi Beach, or the thought of what I was doing, like sitting in that sofa, instead of walking this pesky dog.

On a deeper, and usually less conscious level, being in the present means feeling good with the person I'm with, even if he reminds me of that teacher who used to threaten me, or that cousin who sexually abused me, or that friend who abandoned me when I was four. Now an adult, I may still feel like the small, powerless child when in a situation that seems threatening, meaning I am living, at an emotional level, in the past.

Alex, a man in his fifties, in a secure relationship and with an excellent career, told me how self-critical he often felt, and how this sometimes put him into a state of virtual paralysis when he was expected to carry out a new project, which he knew himself to be perfectly capable of doing. He had, in those moments, become his own mother, while the seven-year-old Alex within himself felt worthless in the face of the criticism and disappointment he felt from her.

In this chapter, I will introduce you to the Time Capsule, during which we will hear more of Alex, and others, and through which you will arrive at a higher level of Emotional Fitness.

The figure gives an idea of how, in simple terms, we develop, how we get stuck, and how we may reconnect with our true emotional self in order to become, once again, who we really are, and so that we can connect with others in a healthier, more positive, way.

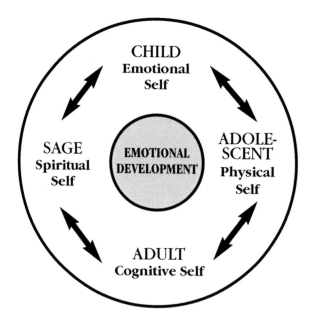

THE CHILD AND THE EMOTIONAL SELF

Our neighbours just had a new baby. Proudly, they showed us little Jessica, a week or two old. She was lively, seeming to show intense interest in what was going on, and in us, the latest of the new people in her life. Her mother told us, "she spends most of her time crying. We have to keep on the move with her, then she keeps quiet." At that moment Jessica puckered up her face, opened her mouth wider than a tiny baby might be expected to, and obliged with a series of yells that could only have been the cry of someone in deep panic and distress. Except, of course, that this was a small baby, not an adult who has learned to contain her emotions, and whose only way to express was to let out a good, healthy bawl. Jessica was just one bundle of emotions. She was not really seeing us as 'adults' or 'her neighbours', or even her parents as her parents.

We can never really delve completely into an understanding of what is going on within the infant, but my guess is that Jessica was experiencing a sensation that, being new (what isn't new when you're a few days old?) led her to express her feelings in the only natural way she could. Maybe she felt hungry, scared, uncomfortable, even for a moment. A moment would be enough for an emotional reaction. Everything, for the small child, is experienced and expressed through the emotions, without constraint, consideration, inhibitions or fear of consequences. This is our core, our emotional selves, who we really are deep inside ourselves.

Jessica will remember none of this when she is four, or forty. When she is four it won't matter at all. When she is forty, she may want to return to who she really is, since, inevitably, she will have moved through so much in her life that she might have questions that lead her to wonder how she got there. In forty years time, that will be her present, and this will be her past. More realistically, Jessica will recall something of her four-year-old experience, and not of her two-week-old one, since by four she will be fully aware of what is going on around her, and will also have collected enough wisdom to understand that some ways of expressing her emotions are less acceptable than others, and that some work better than others.

Unlike Alex, I suspect that Jessica will not look back at the experience of never feeling OK because her mother expressed her disappointment. Jessica will have her own, unique experience, and that, added to her own, already

If you want to change the world, you'd better know what you're doing.

perfectly moulded and unique soul, will make her story like no other that ever has been or will be told.

The first part of the Time Capsule cycle shows that the predominant capability within the child is that of emotion. There are no words for the infant to express those emotions, no language, and no intellectual grasp of what is happening, since there is no experience to help the child to understand. The gathering of experience, accompanied by the ability to make sense of the world around him or her, means that awareness begins very quickly, and that the child learns with amazing speed.

Nevertheless, for the first few years of the human's life it is emotion that rules, since it is emotion that enables the expression of need and the display of satisfactions and frustrations. When a baby feels the desire for his mother's milk, he will not wait politely for feeding time to come around. He wants it now, and he expresses it loudly and clearly. An infant who feels content, if not asleep, will gurgle and smile her pleasure at the stranger who peeks into her crib. If startled or discomforted by a sudden movement, she may screw up her face in an expression of such total distress and dismay that you might be forgiven for believing that her young world had just come to an end.

The point is that there are no inhibitions in her world. She has not learned them yet. Response is immediate and without concern for consequences. This is just how Jessica behaves at this point in her life.

Imagine, now, yourself at that age, just a few weeks old. You have no concerns apart from how you are feeling right now. This is probably a difficult thing to do, since you have no language or consciousness of anything apart from your sensations, and even those are not understandable to you.

Jot down how you might describe yourself as the tiniest infant. This was you in your first stage of life. This is not something that you remember, nor is it anything that you have heard about yourself or seen in photographs. This is what you imagine now might have been going on inside you if only you could have expressed it in words then. _◯◀▬

Jessica might say something like this:

"I like it when I am being moved about, when I feel the swaying and rocking, and when I hear gentle sounds around me. Company is good, these faces that appear and bob about in front of me. Makes me feel comfortable. The best is the comfort I feel when I am close to the breast and get the milk that warms and soothes me. Where is it now? Where is it? I can call for it now. I can do anything I want. I can have what I want. I am free and I am in charge. I can call on the world for what-

ever I need. That diaper feels wet and messy. Why doesn't it get changed now, right now? Shout louder. Idiots! Why don't they get it? About time too. This is the man who holds me safely and makes me smile when he changes my diaper. This feels so much better. I love it here, the attention, the fascination of all the new sights and sounds, the freedom from being encased and in the dark for all that time; although it was a shock at first when I burst out into the light and everything was so much louder. I shudder every time I think about it. Tired now. I'll sleep."

I don't know about you, but Jessica seems to feel totally in the present and totally self-centred. She also appears to feel free, safe and in charge. Babies in that state are powerful beings, even though they appear completely power-less and dependent upon us to love and care for them, attending to all their needs. Whatever we do to them or for them will affect them in some way. And, since their perceptual condition is one of almost pure emotion, we will affect them emotionally. Thus, the emotional being of the infant will gradual-ly be transformed through being suppressed, damaged, discouraged, educat-ed, or in other ways, usually quite unintentionally, depriving the infant of the feelings of freedom, power and self-love.

When Alex told me of his experience as a seven-year-old, he described an occa-sion when his mother berated him for not having cleaned his room up properly. He recalled vividly her shouting at him "you're just a useless little boy aren't you; I can't rely on you to do anything properly," while he thought that he had done everything he was supposed to, and had no idea what was wrong with his room. "I felt totally bewildered," said Alex, "as though nothing I did could ever be good enough for her. It seemed so unfair. I just didn't know what to do. I just stood there and held back the tears until she went out, then I bawled my head off."

Alex, by the time he was seven, had already learned to hold back his emo-tions from others, had already realized his powerlessness, had felt the denial of his freedom to be himself and do what was OK for him, and had already lost at least part of his capacity for self-love. This fragment of memory was just one for Alex. The process for him would have started way before his memory, and before his consciousness allowed him to understand what was happening to him. At age fifty-two, Alex began to make sense of the impact on him right throughout the rest of his life to that stage.

There's nothing new, just different ways of experiencing the same things.

THE ADOLESCENT AND THE PHYSICAL SELF

Remember your teen years? I certainly remember mine, even now, with a mixture of excitement, fear, adventure, rebellion, embarrassment and anger. The excitement came from the connection with new friends, even though I always felt somewhat on the outside, being a member of 'the gang' and the things that we would plan and carry out, and from the emerging Rock'n'Roll phenomenon. The fear came from the prevailing dread of the time, (this was the 1950s – the era of the Cold War) that we were on the edge of being blown into oblivion by an atomic bomb being dropped on London. The adventure came from the freedom that was emerging for me, the trying out of new possibilities in sports and dancing, and the discovery of girlfriends. The rebellion was against my school, the teachers, my father and stepmother, the constraints and the demands that seemed to me totally unrealistic and designed only to thwart me. My embarrassment was about my body, my uncontrolled sexual urges at extraordinary times (often, it seemed, when jumping onto a bus going home from school!) and my inability to express or even to understand, what I was thinking and feeling. The anger, boiling deep inside me and kept there, was directed at my father, God, the world, anyone I could aim at, for the death of my mother and other family members.

I regard all of these perceptions as based on my decreasing ability, as I moved through childhood into adolescence, to access my emotions and the almost overpowering concern with the physical aspects of myself and the world outside me. The preoccupation with the physical self, and by extension the perception of the world as being solely physical, meant that not only was I no longer able to connect to my emotional self, but that I was not yet capable of fully using my mental abilities, even though they had, of course, been developing in early childhood. Despite the fact that I had grasped the English language and could speak it tolerably well by the age of three, and by six had the ability to read well and understand the rudiments of maths, in my teen years I found it hard to concentrate on the trivia I believed they were trying to teach me in school. Playing cricket (yes, this was England) was a different matter. The feel of the leather ball in my hands; the pressure of standing with the bat ready to face a ball coming towards me at a speed faster than I could react to it; these were the things that could hold my attention. Today, I would probably have been summoned to meet with the school psychologist and told I had Attention Deficit Disorder. No, I think I was probably a fairly normal teenager with interests other than what the school and the rest of society believed I should have. My world was a physical, not an intellectual one.

Educators, or rather those who make educational policy, as well as educational psychologists, would do well to understand that children who are moving from a state of emotional to physical connection with themselves and the world, are not exhibiting abnormal behaviour when they don't conform to the school system's requirements of them to connect with the mental side of themselves. The adult-constructed view of education is, in fact, a way in which we learn to cut off important sides of our humanity in favour of a side that is only partially useful to us. In particular, the education and the wider societal system that most of us live in, actively discourages our emotional fitness in favour of a mental and physical approach to fitness, with spiritual fitness (we will talk about that later), becoming confused with religious instruction.

My perspective of adolescence may or may not fit your own experience of it. Write down some of your personal recollections of you in your teens.

Alex was sixteen when his mother died. He recalls his father telling him to do his best to help look after his two younger sisters, and not to let them down, since that was what his mom would expect. Alex felt the burden, not so much of the duties he performed around the house, but of the responsibility for 'getting them right'. He was constantly imagining his mother standing over him, checking up. Even though his father was fairly easy-going, Alex couldn't shake off this feeling.

When he thought about it, many years afterwards, Alex realized that he compensated for this by doing things that his mother had never been involved in. He took up baseball pretty seriously, taking part in his local league and gaining a strong reputation as a pitcher. His dad occasionally came to watch a game, and Alex remembers the pride he felt as his dad nodded at a good play. He started skiing with a group of school buddies and delighted in his popularity as he became proficient on skis and with the bawdy songs they would chant on the way home.

"I had learned to cope by being good at things," said Alex. "I was vaguely aware of feeling ashamed and guilty about my mom, for some reason that I didn't want to look at, and even about my dad, for enjoying the things I was doing. But mostly, I was just having a good time. I got on well with my sisters, although they later told me I bullied them. I was just trying to get them to take some responsibility for doing stuff around the house. I tried never to think about mom. My

Who do you want to be when you grow up?

dad hardly ever mentioned her. I know that she haunted me though."

It seems that Alex was denying the emotional self of his early childhood, and not yet ready to enter fully the more logical, cognitive self. He was content, for the time being, to stay with the world of sensation, to be and to test out his physical self.

Alex was an adolescent at this time, exhibiting adolescent behaviour, just as Jessica is an infant, exhibiting exactly what is normal in infants. As we grow into adulthood we lose and retain aspects of childhood and adolescence. The extent to which we do that is the extent to which we are able to mature into a fully functioning, healthy individual. The adolescent's desire for material things that will enhance his or her appearance and desirability is a natural part of the growing-up process. When this physical manifestation of desire is frustrated, in other words when a person does not become satisfied that he or she is desirable, there will remain an insatiable need for the material things in life. The car, the clothes, the 'stuff' that people collect; the addictions of alcohol, drugs, sex, smoking; the co-dependent relationships that become the norm; these are usually the results of a 'frozen' adolescent desire that has never been fully satisfied. Until we acknowledge and support the adolescent within us, we cannot escape from those needs and transform the frustration into something more positive for us. We might say that the whole of the consumer society is still in an adolescent state. Possibly, like the trauma an adult experiences before he or she decides to 'grow up', our 21st century western culture has needed the trauma of terrorism before it can grow out of its adolescent need to collect more and more physical possessions.

When I met Alex, he was stuck in two main areas in his life. He could not seem to achieve the success he felt was really due to him in his work, and despite having a good salary, he never felt financially secure. Those two areas were mirrored by the emotional scarring he had received from his mother, and the search for physical accomplishment that never quite satisfied his craving for love and acknowledgment.

THE ADULT AND THE COGNITIVE SELF

Alex, like most of the rest of the adult human race, especially the male adult, survived, in his case relatively successfully, by living largely in the realm of cognition. Women tend to retain more of their emotional and physical selves, since their survival mode is more dependent upon those, and since, as girls, they are encouraged more than their male counterparts to express their emotions. This works both for and against them, depending on which parts remain whole and what has been damaged along the way. It might be worth pausing for a while here to explore some of the gender differences. The differences are both innate and socialized into us, although I will not join the 'nature or nurture' debate except to say that this is the mix that makes us who we are.

Men tend to focus more on the logical and cognitive since that is what is most often required of them in the race for survival. Early humans were never very advantaged when it came to speed and strength over their enemies and prey; so they used their guile to hunt. The males were predominantly the hunters, while the females, since they had to suckle their young, would tend to remain with them in and around the relative safety of their caves. Despite major changes for women over the past fifty years, the previous 30,000 years has had its effect on how we think!

Men have also been traditionally regarded as being 'weak' if they express their feelings, while the adolescent trait of physical prowess is seen as 'manly' in most societies and communities. Women, on the other hand, are more highly regarded when they express their emotions (unless this, of course, is in the 'men's' world of work, when they learn to act more like 'men'). Women understand that having and expressing their feelings is acceptable, at least in their own circle of female friends, and that an expression of their physical side is also acceptable and indeed, sexually attractive. There is, therefore, less reliance on the cognitive side in order for women to survive.

Having said that, cognition, or the thinking, mental capacity is the predominant state within which both men and women live in our society. This has become more pronounced over the past century or so, since the Industrial Revolution and, in particular, over the past couple of decades, since the computer and information revolution. I believe that our minds have been stretched more quickly over the past twenty years than at any time in the history of the human race. Unfortunately, this has only served to shrink some of the other sides of ourselves, although there is no need for this – we will not reach the extent of the mind's capacity for thinking for a long time yet. Meanwhile we have far more capacity for the feeling, intuitive, spiritual and creative areas that will probably take us beyond our logical abilities when we become open to them.

Whatever you do will have unexpected consequences.

For now, my proposition is that the normal adult state is that of cognition. I am not attempting to arrive by some other route at the very essence of Descartes' philosophical belief *cogito ergo sum* (I think, therefore I am), but rather to see that thinking, and to a large extent the doing from that thinking, are the central activities of the adult human. That human thinking is unique is evident from our invention and use of language in every human society. In teaching our language to children we ask them to develop their cognitive powers. It is inescapable that we become immersed in thinking. Our minds, even when asleep, are alert and working. Step 7, Dreamtime, explores that further.

When I said that Alex had survived by living in his cognition, this was literally true. At the age of 23, he attempted to kill himself. Alex had left home by then, had started a job in sales that demanded considerable travel, and found himself spending a large amount of his spare time alone. He started feeling inadequate, turned to alcohol for solace, became depressed, and took an overdose of sleeping pills. During the aftermath of this episode he received some counselling, which brought on his feelings of inadequacy and guilt. One day, leaving a counselling session, he made a conscious decision. "This is driving me crazy," he said to himself. "I'm just going to get on with my life and stop feeling sorry for myself. I'll concentrate on doing my job, getting the best sales results of the department, and enjoy life." It was, in a way, a real wake-up call to Alex. He knew that he no longer wanted to feel depressed, nor did he want to drink, and that the only way for him was to submerge his negative feelings. Sometimes, as in the case of Alex, it takes an act of will to do this; usually it is an unconscious, automatic kind of defense mechanism to avoid being hurt.

The result, for Alex, was that he survived by thinking, by being logical about what he wanted and how he would get it. A longer-term result was that, when he was ready, Alex recognized that he was stuck by having denied his feelings, and that, in order to go beyond survival and into fulfillment, he needed to return to them in a different, more mature way.

Since thinking is, by my definition, the adult response, and one that is limited because of that, it follows that the normal adult response is a limiting and usually passive one, however active the thinking may be. Reading all the self-improvement books in the world is essentially a passive process, as is going to listen to the 'self-development experts' willing to tell you how to live your life in exchange for your money. We need to deal with things on a personal, interactive and dynamic basis by reaching into the different aspects of our child, adolescent and adult self, and discovering the sage within. In other words, we can become our own guru.

How does my description fit in with your image of yourself? Take a few minutes to consider how you now mainly 'inhabit your world'. Think specifically of a recent experience of yours, something that took place no more than 48 hours ago. Jot down the experience and say how you reacted to it.

THE SAGE AND THE SPIRITUAL SELF

The fourth, and ultimate stage in our development is one that few people take, and even those who do, touch for no more than a small proportion of time. This is the part that we need to concentrate on with more consciousness than the other three stages. The rest has been largely an unconscious, normal process of natural growth and socialization, tinged with specific, sometimes traumatic experiences.

The spiritual self is one that only you can define for yourself. How would you define it? Write down your sense or understanding of what spirituality means to you.

Here is my approach to spirituality, and it may differ markedly from yours. Since, for each of us, we are both right, because we each have the quality of uniqueness, the question arises, 'how may those two (possibly divergent) views relate to each other so that there is congruence between them?'

My understanding of the spiritual self is in the moment of reconnection. That is, when we reconnect with our (child) emotional self, using our (adolescent) physical attributes, and our (adult) cognitive self. That is the moment at which we become whole, when we arrive at a point of inner wisdom and knowing. We are, in that moment, the sage, or crone, and have reached into the essence of who we really are.

Alex is a fine example of someone who achieved that. This is some of his story and part of a conversation we had:

Warren: You've shared a lot with me, Alex. Can you put together what you now understand to be the essence of where you are?
Alex: I've been married for nearly 25 years and I have a good job; yet I'm still not sure that my wife really loves me, and I don't feel that I've succeeded as much as I could have in my work. Even with this job that pays well, I don't feel secure

financially. I really need to understand why I feel one way, when at the same time I know it's nonsense.

W: *Is that the understanding that you need to have? It seems to me that you have a good understanding of yourself already from what you have talked about over the past few weeks.*

A: *Maybe so. Yes, but I still feel stuck and self-critical. OK, so I feel stuck and self-critical, even though there is no reason for it now. It seems that I'm stuck with old feelings of guilt and inadequacy.*

W: *Does it seem like that to you?*

A: *Yes, it does. When I feel bad, it's almost as though I am being a child instead of a fifty-two-year-old man. I have exactly the same sensations.*

W: *This is something you want to change?*

A: *You bet I do; but I don't know how. Even if I understand it, it doesn't go away.*

W: *I'd like to get a stronger picture of how you feel stuck and inadequate. Can you give me a real example of a recent event, something that happened maybe just a day or two ago, when you felt like that?*

A: *Let me see. Well, just yesterday. I don't know if it's what you want. It was a conversation I had with my boss.*

W: *Alex, if you feel it fits, it will be exactly right. I'm simply looking for a snap-shot, if you like, of your most recent experience when you felt stuck and inadequate.*

A: *Well, there I go again, feeling inadequate in giving you an example. (Laughs). Anyway, yesterday, not long after I had arrived at the office, my boss walked in.*

W: *Alex, could you put yourself into the present with this. In other words, say it like it's happening now. You're in the office and your boss walks in...*

A: *I'm in the office and my boss walks in. He's the COO of the corporation and I'm directly responsible to him for the major projects under my care. He's a very 'hands off' guy, and I have a lot of freedom to get on with my work. But when he comes in, I immediately think that something's wrong, that I must have screwed up somewhere. My mind starts racing and I think it must be a project that I haven't really begun yet, and I should at least have produced an initial outline for. This is before he's even said anything, beyond good morning and inconsequential stuff. Then he asks me about it – about the project, I mean, and I know I was right. He says, "I've been speaking with John," (who's a new technical director), "and I'd like him to work with you on that project. It would be a good way for him to show what he can do. Do you mind?" I just felt like he'd given me a roasting for not having started on the project and that he didn't believe that I could do it well enough. At the same time, I'm thinking, 'of course that makes sense, and it'll help me as well as being an opportunity for John.' John, by the way, is a great guy. I helped to appoint him and his work won't directly impinge on mine once he gets into it. It makes total sense that he understands some of the processes of these projects in order to help him do his job better.*

W: *Let me see if I understand this. You are in your office when your boss walks in. You immediately feel that you have done something wrong. When he suggests that John works with you, this reinforces your feeling of inadequacy, even though you understand, and agree with, the reason for his suggestion. From what you have said, I also understand that you have been stuck in getting this project off the ground and feel that you are being reprimanded for this.*

A: *Yes, that's about it. Seems pretty stupid doesn't it? Then to compound it, I say something like, "I just need a day or two to get the information together, then I can get on with the project fine. I don't think it would help to have John work on this until I have got it going." Then he says, "I think it will help both you and him, Alex. You sound a little defensive about this, I don't know what you're worried about." I didn't – I don't – know what to say and it kind of gets left there, with me feeling even more stupid. I'll bet it does to you too.*

W: *Not to me, Alex. It seems like your emotions and your logic are having a battle, and that is very common. You've now told me that you became defensive and that your boss remarked on this, so that you felt stupid. This, then, is an example of something you would like to change.*

A: *It certainly is. If only I knew how.*

W: *What I would like now is for you to give me another fragment of an experience, another snapshot; this time, the earliest one you can recall, something from your childhood. Just see what pops into your head, and again, tell me as though it is happening now.*

A: *The one that comes up straight away is the one I think I told you about when we first met. I'm about seven years old. I'm standing in my bedroom. I think it's in the evening, perhaps on a Saturday. I don't know why I think so, but it seems like that.*

W: *Tell me what is happening.*

When you meet your sage, you have met your inner child.

A: *My mom is standing over me. She seems so tall, although I don't think she was very big. She is shouting at me, telling me I'm useless. "You're a useless little boy," she says, "you can't do anything properly. I just can't rely on you can I?" She's angry with me for not cleaning my room up properly, and I'm thinking 'but I did clean it up; what does she want? What's wrong with it? It's not fair. Nothing I do is any good for her.' I feel the tears welling up. Thank goodness she leaves the room before I burst out crying. When she's gone, I throw myself onto the bed and bawl for ages. At the unfairness I guess. I'm angry at her, and I'm angry at myself for being no good.*

W: *You seem to have a very vivid recollection of that seven-year-old Alex, and a strong connection to him. Stay with him for a moment. What I want you to do now is to go into the room with him. Imagine that you, now, the adult Alex, can go to visit that seven-year-old Alex bawling his head off on his bed. And young Alex can see you, has you to himself. What does young Alex want from the fifty-two-year-old Alex? Is there anything he wants to ask, or to say?*

A: *Oh boy. What does little Alex want? He wants to know he's OK. He wants some comfort and reassurance.*

W: *How does he ask for that?*

A: *He says... (cries quietly for a while). He says, "please hold me. Just hold me and tell me what I've done that's so wrong. Tell me why mom is so angry with me all the time." (Cries, this time more loudly and longer). I'm sorry.*

W: *I wonder why you feel you have to say that you're sorry for expressing your emotions. Stay with young Alex and answer his questions. He wants to know what he's done wrong, and why his mom is so angry with him. And he wants you to hold him. Can you do that?*

A: *Yes, I can do that. I can hold him. Oh boy, I can hold him for a long time. And I can tell him. "You've done nothing wrong. You've done your best. In fact, you've done a great job, especially for a seven-year-old. I'm proud of you. As for mom, you know what, I have a feeling that she's not well, and that she's not happy. I wish I knew what her problem was – is – but I have a pretty good idea that she really loves you, and is just very unhappy with her life." That's what I have to tell him.*

W: *How does young Alex feel at this point?*

A: *He feels a lot better. He feels great being held. (Laughs). He feels like he's being squashed, but it's a wonderful feeling. For the first time, he feels he's not alone. And for the first time, he has someone to tell him he's OK. And he is getting a different insight into his mom. You know, I need to ask my dad about her. We've never really discussed her much, at least not about how she might have been feeling when I was young. But then, I've never asked him.*

W: *Sounds like you want to do this for young Alex. Maybe take him with you.*

A: *Absolutely. Though I won't tell my dad that!*

W: *Let's see now. You have told me how, the other day, your boss came into your office, and you felt that you had done something wrong, and then felt inadequate for your response. Now you have told me of being shouted at by your mom for being useless, and you have spoken to that small Alex and he now feels OK, and not alone, and understood, and he also understands more about his mom. Now can you ask young Alex, from his new understanding, if there is anything he wants to say to you, the adult Alex, as he has witnessed the incident with your boss yesterday.*

A: *He'd say, "Don't be an idiot Alex." No, he wouldn't say that, but I probably would. Young Alex tells me that my boss is not my mom, and I'm not seven any more, and in any case, that kid now feels a heck of a lot better. He says to me, "You're OK. I'm proud of what you've achieved. And you can have a big hug any time. Oh, and your boss thinks you're fine, but doesn't understand that you feel fearful."*

W: *Well, you have a pretty powerful ally there, Alex. Now I'd like you to go ahead in time. You have been in a time capsule, visiting a tiny fragment of time in your present, then in the past. Now get back into that time capsule and go forward, say a year from now. Tell me what's happening; what do you see, what are you doing, what are you feeling?*

A: *I can see myself back in the office. It feels OK, because I like the work, and it's fulfilling to me. The funny thing is, I can picture myself right now having a conversation on the phone with my wife. I'm telling her about this project I'm working on and how successful it is. And she is telling me how pleased she is for me. Then she's telling me about something she has been doing. Oh boy, I realize that we never talk like this. I thought we had a good relationship, but we never talk about most of the things that are really important to us. No, that's not true, she does, but I don't. I don't listen to her properly, and I don't say much about what's important to me.*

W: *So, Alex, you have had a glimpse into your future. Is this how you would like it to be?*

A: *Well, as far as it goes. Yes, you know, if that is just a glimpse, it's a great one.*

FAMILY = Father and Mother, I love you.

I could certainly live with that.

W: *Very well, then. Is there something that you now want to ask of Alex, in that future scene, in your office, talking with your wife about things that are important to you both, you feeling good about yourself?*

A: *Can you say that again?*

W: *Of course, and much more simply. Is there something that you now want to ask of the future Alex?*

A: *I want to say to him, "well done", but I think there is something I want to ask. Let me see. I want to ask, "how does it really feel? Do you feel complete?" There may be more, but that's it for now.*

W: *And what does Alex from the future answer?*

A: *It feels good. I don't know about complete. I'm beginning to understand that this is a constant journey; what's that about the journey not being the destination? But it feels kind of exhilarating to be sharing my thoughts and feelings with my wife, and to be proud of my achievements. You know, I love my wife, but I don't think I really show it. Not in the way that she'd like.*

W: *Anything else you want to ask of future Alex before he has to get on with his work, and his life?*

A: *I'd like to ask what took him so long. And he takes a long look at me and tells me that it started now, when I stopped feeling sorry for myself as a kid, and began to see myself, and others around me, differently. When I realized I was OK, it was OK to cry, OK to feel angry, and OK for doing my best, which was better than OK, I began to ... what? I guess I began to be myself, not to hide myself under the pretense of not being able to do things, when I know I can. Wow!*

W: *Wow indeed. What do you think you want to do next?*

A: *I want to go and take my wife out to dinner and talk to her. And listen to her too. Yes, I need to listen to her a lot more than I have. And I want to talk to my dad, although it probably doesn't matter so much now. What's more important is that I keep talking to young Alex. And tomorrow, I'll have a word with my boss, and tell him that, I don't know, I was caught off guard and that, of course it's fine to work with John and I'll welcome the collaboration.*

Make a few notes about your understanding of the process used in the interaction between Alex and me, and of your thoughts about the nature of the stages that Alex went through from the start to the finish of the process.

THE 10 TIME CAPSULE STAGES

The conversation with Alex was an example of the use of the Time Capsule, the fourth step in Inner Balancing. The stages are simple, although their use will depend a great deal on the individual and the issues being raised. As with any of these tools therefore, they need considerable practice before they work as well as they can.

Here are the basic stages in the Time Capsule process. I'll go through the stages as though you are listening to someone else, although you can of course, be the person talking about your personal experiences. As always, it helps to have an Emotional Fitness Instructor taking you through this process.

1. Decide if the Time Capsule is appropriate. Is the speaker sharing with you an experience that is part of a pattern in his or her life? This will become very clear to you if you are listening well, and you can check this out simply by asking if the experience or the feeling is a familiar one.
2. Ask the speaker to describe the most recent experience (within the last 24 hours if possible), when the same or a similar feeling emerged.
3. Summarize this (you are using Listening Power constantly).
4. Ask the speaker to travel back in time and discover the first experience that comes up from his or her earliest memories. Ask the speaker to describe that experience as though it were happening now, using the present tense.
5. Summarize what you have heard.
6. Invite the speaker to have a dialogue with the present and past self. You now need to use your creativity and all your powers of listening. Ask yourself, "who needs the most help here, the adult or the child?" Remember that your task is to help the speaker discover his or her own inner wisdom and support, not to get in the way with your own. Yours is in the process you are offering, and in your skills in using Listening Power and the Time Capsule.
7. Offer a summary of the dialogue you have heard.
8. Ask the speaker to take the Time Capsule and travel into the future, say a year from now. Invite him or her to describe what is going on and what the future experience feels like.

I think, therefore I am. I feel, therefore I'm human.

9. Ask the speaker to have another dialogue, this time with the future self. Perhaps there are questions to ask and answers to be found. This is a conversation between the present and the future, and sometimes the past self, with your assistance as an onlooker facilitating the process, for the speaker to discover his or her own inner wisdom.

10. Finally, ask the speaker to make a summary of what the experience has been like and what action the speaker wants to take.

Now try the Time Capsule. With your skills in Listening Power, and your practice in Learning from Experience and the Lifescale, you will have become ready to work with the Time Capsule. Be aware of the fact that this is a powerful process, and that the person you are listening to is a very precious person who will be putting a great deal of trust in you. Honour that person for what he or she is sharing with you.

Invite your sharing partner. Explain how you want to work with him or her and that you are trying this out for the first time, inviting their comments at the end. Relax, concentrate, and enjoy the process. When you have completed the Time Capsule, make a note of your experience, with any comments that your sharing partner has made about the process. If you have access to someone who is an Emotional Fitness Instructor or is learning, ask him or her to facilitate the Time Capsule with you. When you have shared, make a note of your own experience here. ✐◁▬

The Time Capsule is a powerful process because it allows us to make the connection, not only between the past, present, and future, but also between the mental, physical and emotional part of ourselves. When our adult meets and recognizes our adolescent and our child self, we become whole at last. That wholeness, that bringing together of the pieces in our fragmented life, is, in my opinion, the discovery of our spiritual self.

My rediscovery of love came when I uncovered my early childhood experience. Up until then, I had been trying to recreate what I had believed I had lost, in the process putting extreme pressure on those from whom I had sought love. Neither my first, nor my second wife, nor any other woman, could ever have filled the gap in my life. The same was true of friends, and from men whom I had looked up to. Seldom would they be able to sustain, in my mind, the qualities of deserved loyalty that I had invested in them. When at last I understood that I had never lost the love I had felt as a child, I was able to offer the love I had locked up within me. My emotional child self had remained dormant because he was so scared of being abandoned and hurt again. One Time Capsule did not do that, but it did open the door for me to continue what I had started with John Heimler.

The journey is a constant one.

One Saturday morning, about seven years ago, my wife Nicole, and I were getting ready to leave our apartment to go for our regular weekly breakfast at a local bagel and coffee shop. Something happened, something was said; I cannot remember what, but I do remember feeling upset and angry. We stood in the elevator glaring at each other, and I felt that the weekend was already spoiled, ready to blame Nicole for making me feel bad. I was fifty-five and I felt like a five-year-old.

We had our breakfast, without much joy, and walked back home. I went to lie on the bed, still feeling miserable. "I have the tools to deal with this," I said to myself. "I'll do a Time Capsule on myself." Even as I thought that, another part of me thought that this was nonsense. It was cut and dried; Nicole was at fault, and I didn't understand why she acted this way, but it was nothing to do with me. I recall smiling at myself, having this inner argument. "OK," I thought, "I'll do a Time Capsule and see what happens." I still didn't believe it would make any difference. This was my conversation with myself.

"What happened?"

"We were going for breakfast. I was looking forward to it. Then Nicole said something to me, and I felt put down, felt as though I had done something wrong. After that, it seemed as though the weekend was going to be ruined, and I spent a miserable time at breakfast, not talking much."

"What's the earliest memory that comes up for you?"

"This isn't going to work. OK, OK, let's see. I'm four. My mother is ironing and I'm getting ready to go to bed. This has nothing to do with anything."

"Just get on with it."

"Right. I'm wearing my pyjamas. I've kissed grandma and Daddy Bender good night. Now I'm going to mommy. She is standing behind the ironing board and I reach up my arms to her. She leans forward, and the iron falls off the board. It crashes down on my foot."

As I say this out loud to myself, I actually feel a sharp pain in my big toe on my left foot. I hold the toe for a while until the pain, and my surprise, subside. I go back to my Time Capsule, now feeling that this is serious and that something is happening.

"When the iron comes crashing down on your foot, how do you feel?"

Laughter is contagious. Spread it around.

"Well, I start crying. It's very painful, but I'm also feeling hurt and upset because she wasn't careful, and I was just wanting a kiss from her."

"Anything else?"

"She seems so far from me, up there, towering above me from behind the ironing board. There's no way I can get to her."

"OK. Now imagine that you are there with that little four-year-old Warren. What does he want from you? What can you offer to him?"

A wave of emotion surges through me. I can only describe it as a shudder that seems to run right through my body. I start to cry, as though a great release of energy is coming out of me. After a little while, I am able to answer myself.

"He wants some comfort from me, and some explanation. I tell him, it was an accident; she didn't mean to hurt you, she was just clumsy, she loves you."

I cry again, this time gently, feeling a great sense of relief and joy, knowing this to be true, and knowing what was coming.

"And when little Warren sees you this morning, having that argument with Nicole, what does he want to say to you?"

It is hard for me to get the words out, since I am feeling quite emotional, but I make myself say them out loud.

"She didn't mean to hurt you, she was just clumsy, she loves you. Haven't you learned anything over the past fifty years?"

A surge of love, tinged with some embarrassment at my idiocy, and pride at my own success, flows through me.

"So both young Warren and you now know that you are loved, that sometimes the person who loves you can be clumsy, and that you act in a hurt way, as though they don't love you."

I do not need to respond.

"Now take yourself forward in time, a year from now. Tell me what you are doing."

"It's another Saturday. Nicole and I are going out to breakfast together. It feels comfortable. We are very close, and enjoy each other's company. I am able to respond to her in a loving way even if she is telling me something that I don't like to hear, because I know that she is very direct, has a particular style, which is exactly one of the things I love about her, and I can look after my four-year-old self if those hurt feelings come up."

I get up from the bed and walk to the living-room where Nicole is sitting. I ask her to listen to me, and tell her what I have just done. As I bring her my feelings and describe my experience, she responds in a similar way. It is one more moment of sharing that brings us to greater understanding and enhances our *relationship. To this day, when I get a similar feeling from something that Nicole says, I picture that moment, so many years ago, of my mother dropping the iron onto my foot, and know that she loved me at that moment, as Nicole does now. It makes my response very different. Of course, I sometimes still forget, and have to go through it all over again.*

I love these Saturday morning breakfasts with my wife now as a highlight of my week. Not only are they a testament to our relationship; they are a reminder that Inner Balancing works for me, too, in a very real way.

CONNECTING WITH OUR CHILD AND OUR ADOLESCENT

So far, most of the connection has been between the adult self and the child. That is not only because the inner, emotional experience and potential wisdom of the child is usually where we will gain a new understanding, but also because the root cause of our current behaviour rests within our very earliest encounters with life. The child is witness to, or actually experiences, almost everything in some form or another that will have a lifelong impact. This is usually unconscious, which is why we don't understand why we do things the way we do, or why 'things happen to us' the way they always seem to.

When, in later life, we suffer the same feelings of being stuck, or of always getting into difficult situations, or have problems with relationships, the chances are we are dealing with some previous, probably very early, frozen need. For example, if you regularly have a feeling of abandonment, or rejection, when someone you care about even hints that they may be angry with you, or might not want to be around you for a while, then you probably had an early and distressing experience of someone close to you leaving. The emotional impact on us of such a trauma, especially when it is ignored or unnoticed by the adults around us at the time, may leave us with a need, frozen in time, that never leaves us, unless and until we reconnect with, and heal our hurt child.

In the case of Alex, he had become able to create a safer place for himself in relation to his boss and his wife, through discovering that he could support and heal the small boy feeling under attack from his mother. In my own case, I found that, by visualizing and connecting with myself at four years old, I could change the way I felt and behaved when feeling under

Talking to yourself is the first sign of sanity.

attack from someone I loved.

While most of the feelings we have as adults are rooted in our childhood, some come from events experienced in adolescence, a highly significant growth period in our lives. In my model, the adolescent lives largely in the physical realm. Without strong, positive and loving parental support, expressing emotions is no longer a safe or validating thing to do, so we are likely to shut those down as much as possible. Thinking logically and expressing ourselves intellectually isn't really that cool either, nor are we too interested in using our mental capacities, although we are still going through an immense amount of, largely enforced, learning.

Physically, things are much more absorbing. How we look, and what we wear is intensely important. Where we hang out has considerable relevance. What we do, and who we do it with marks us as in or out with the crowd. The stuff we have says who we are. The apparently superficial has vital significance to a teen. It is not hard to see that, beneath the desire to be seen as wanting, no, needing physical things to be just right, lies a huge emotional cauldron ready to burst at any moment. The result of all the physical changes and desires, together with, from the teen's perspective, the total inability of parents and other adults to understand anything important, is the urge towards rebellion.

When the rebel within us receives no satisfaction or is crushed during its time of natural blooming, we are setting ourselves up for later difficulties. The adult rebel is potentially much more dangerous than the adolescent one. When the frozen need is that of an adolescent, be prepared for later mischief. The repressed teen may become a danger to him or herself, or to others in later life.

Angela was by her own account, a happy and well-rounded child. When she was twelve, Angela's father was killed in a road accident, and her world was shattered. While this was a tragedy, the real longer-term trauma for Angela was that her mother coped by refusing to grieve (openly at any rate), or discuss what had happened. She also became highly protective of Angela, her only child, by not allowing her to go out. Angela's mother remarried less than two years later, to a divorced man with two sons a little older than Angela, who lived with their mother. While Angela's stepfather was not unkind to her, he seemed to believe that it was his duty to protect her from drugs, sexual promiscuity, and other of the dangers that he perceived would certainly befall children unless they were closely monitored.

When I met Angela, she was in her late thirties. Her marriage had recently broken down, and she was sharing custody of her two daughters with her ex-husband. She had first told me that the main reason their marriage had failed was her husband's indifference to her, and his infidelity. Later she confided that it was she who had engaged in multiple affairs, and was even now apparently unable to stop what had become a sexual addiction, mainly for older married men.

When we first did a Time Capsule, Angela went, not surprisingly, to the moment she heard of her father's sudden death. She began to make sense of her addiction for older men, but later, when we did another Time Capsule, she returned to a time when her stepfather caught her secretly preparing to leave the house one evening to meet her friends. I asked Angela to describe the event to me, as though it were happening now.

A   *"I'm in my bedroom, putting on some make-up. I'd told mom I had a school assignment to finish, and then I was going to bed early, but I planned to get out from my bedroom window. It was really easy, because I had a balcony that was just above the back yard, with a great tree you could climb down. Anyway, there's this knock on the door. I'd locked it. It's my stepfather, and he asks if I'm OK. Well, I don't know what to do. I just call out that I'm fine, and he asks me why I've locked the door, and he wants to talk to me or something. I go to the door and open it a little, just put my head around and say, 'I'm getting ready for bed now.' But he doesn't believe me, and pushes the door open. He sees I'm all dressed, with lipstick on. Boy, he really goes for me; tells me to wipe it all off and get downstairs. Then, in front of mom, he lectures me for an hour."*

W   *"How are you feeling in that moment?"*

A   *"I hate him. This is so unfair. I just want to get out of this place, out of the gloom and doom, and this prison they keep me in. I just want to go out and have some fun with my friends. It's not as though I'm going to rob a bank or do anything wrong. Why don't they trust me?"*

W   *"If you can be in the room with Angela at fifteen years old, what does she say to you?"*

A   *"She says .... she just looks at me and she asks what's going on, what is happening to my life, why doesn't anybody care? And why don't they let me just be me?"*

W   *"How do you answer her?"*

Everything always goes according to plan. It just may not be your plan.

A   *"You can be you. And I know it's not fair. You want to go and have fun. But*
      you know they do care for you. They don't understand you, but they do want
      to protect you. (Long silence). And I care for you too. But I know I haven't
      protected you. I've let you run wild and haven't shown you that I cared for
      you. I see that I've let you rule me for the last ten years. All you want is to be
      understood and cared for, and I've let you down, just like my mom did. Just
      like my stepdad. And just like my dad. The thing I realize now is that they
      all cared for you, and I didn't care for you myself".

In this excerpt, Angela, the adolescent, was concerned about her physical
world; her friends, her looks, her desire to go out and 'have fun'. When this
was denied her, she construed this as the denial of who she was. Her suppressed natural growth emerged later, when she felt powerful enough to do
what she wanted without the watchful eye of her parents holding her back,
but not powerful enough to watch over herself. The strength of her adolescent, physical self took over her cognitive, adult self, and she was unable to
access her child, emotional being. When she did so, through exploring her
past and present connections with the help of the Time Capsule, she was
able to move ahead in a much more positive way with her life.

Having read more about the Time Capsule, you may be ready to explore
more deeply some of the significant connections in your own life. If you are
in touch with someone else who is familiar with Inner Balancing, ask them
to work with you. If not, be your own guide, writing down your own experiences and your own dialogue with your present, your past and your future
self. This way you can become your own sage, accessing the wisdom within
you and finding another route to your growing Emotional Fitness.

Before moving on to the next step, review your personal learning contract again. Make notes in your journal to describe how you are doing now.

Your emotion is your energy in motion.

STEP 5: GROUP DIALOGUE
WE'RE IN THIS TOGETHER

I have found the best way to give advice to your children is to find out what they want and then advise them to do it.

Harry S. Truman
(1884-1972)
33rd U.S. President

We cannot learn from one another until we stop shouting at one another – until we speak quietly enough so that our words can be heard as well as our voices.

Richard M. Nixon
(1913-1994)
37th U.S. President

My first book on Inner Balancing, *Achieving Personal Success,* was written over a long period of time, ten years to be exact, during which the whole process was opening up to me. I started the book in 1984 and it was finally published in 1995. I would write a section or a chapter, and then I would put the writing aside in order to try out my ideas and develop them further. As I wrote, I would learn more. As I learned more, I would recognize how much there was still to discover.

There were long periods of time when I simply stopped writing, feeling that I had come to an impasse or that it took too much time and energy. After all, I had a busy and industrious life. I also knew at some level that I was avoiding facing some difficult and important decisions in my life. The most important and painful one was the knowledge that I was in a second marriage that was, and felt untenable. I understood that this was so, but did not understand how I could change the comfortable lifestyle I had become accustomed to, having already done this once before and started from scratch financially. How could I go through it all over again, even though it could never be as hard as the first time, when this entailed living apart from my children?

By 1992 I had, indeed, made the change. This was precipitated partly by the death, at the end of 1990, of John Heimler. I decided to visit Calgary, where Heimler had taught for many years. I reconnected there with the woman whom I had met in 1984, and who had, unwittingly, inspired me to begin the book, and who was to become my third wife. I was ready, at last, to open myself up to an unconditional love. I moved to France, where Nicole joined me. Later we lived in England, and two years after that settled in Canada.

But in 1992, I still had my incomplete manuscript lying in a drawer, while I spent much of my working time running leadership training courses for senior and aspiring managers in large corporations. During one such training course, I demonstrated the Group Dialogue. It was near the end of the week-long course, and the group of fifteen management trainees had been highly motivated and enthusiastic. I sought one more person to be prepared to present an issue and a facilitator to run the process.

"I'll facilitate if you'll present," was the challenge one of the group threw at me. I agreed, and chose to talk about the unfinished book that was about two-thirds complete after eight years. The outcome, to cut this story short, was that I gave myself a deadline. If I had not completed the book by the end of the year (it was then September), I would drop the whole project. I had seen the power of the Group Dialogue many times. This was the first time that it had such a radical effect on me, although it was not to be the last. I completed *Achieving Personal Success,* in its first draft, by the deadline I had given myself. Nicole and I moved to Calgary at the end of 1993, and I spent the next six months preparing the book for publication, finishing another manuscript that I had been working on for even longer (*Bender's Box,* more of which in Storytime), creating a complete manuscript of another novel, and writing three more management development books that were published over the next year or two.

The Group Dialogue is the fifth of the nine steps of Inner Balancing. Every single one of them has worked for me, as it has for many hundreds, probably thousands, of other people over the past few years. As an extension of Listening Power, the Group Dialogue is a process that transforms the way people in groups can listen to, hear, understand, accept, and respond to each other. Imagine this happening in the workplace, in families, or anywhere where people gather together with the intention of trying to communicate more openly and honestly in order to function positively. Imagine how this can change relationships for the better, and inspire people to positive, creative action.

Emotional Fitness in groups is an elusive quality. Inner Balancing helps to provide that Emotional Fitness, and none more so than the Group Dialogue. It was, in fact, my interest in helping dysfunctional groups to perform together more effectively and healthily, that provided the basis for the development of this process. Once again, it was my collaboration with John Heimler that was the inspiration.

Towards the latter days of my involvement with Heimler, I was working mostly with groups and teams of professional community workers, social workers, leaders and managers. One afternoon, while part of a facilitation class with Heimler, I mentioned to him that most of the work we had been doing had focussed on individual therapy, while I was involved more and more in working with groups interested in their personal and professional development. "Why don't we adapt your methods to groups?" I asked him.

He thought for a moment. We were a small group, just six of us, and with hardly any hesitation, he said, in his rich Hungarian accent, "why not? First we will have a presenter, then we will all ask clarifying questions, then we will all summarize, and finally, we will give our ideas of how we would handle the situation, putting ourselves into the shoes of the presenter."

We tried it, and from the first, the process was so powerful that we continued to use it. Soon I started to use it myself with different groups, began to modify and refine it, and came up with the Group Dialogue. I have used it successfully in personal development classes, with workplace teams, with groups of corporate executives, and of course in all of the Emotional Fitness courses. Others have used it with their families, friends and neighbours, often as a mediation tool.

One man who had completed an Emotional Fitness course suggested to his five brothers and their wives that they try it. Steve and his brothers and sisters-in-law got together once a month, usually to play cards and drink beer. Steve's mother had become quite frail, and was increasingly needing full-time care, and Steve had been having little success in getting anyone from the family to discuss how to handle it. This was nothing new; the family seldom talked about anything that seemed, to Steve, to matter. Steve announced to his brothers that he had just tried a great new way of talking and solving problems (he thought this was the best way to describe it), that they could do while just sitting around the table. He asked everyone to think of something they might like to talk about, something that had a personal impact on them. Then he invited someone to talk, while everyone else just listened. It was little surprise that the first person started talking about their mother. Steve, with some difficulty, managed to get the others to listen and to ask questions, rather than all jump into their own ideas on the subject. He

It's hard to shake hands when your fist is clenched.

emphasized the 'rules of the game' and kept asking the others just to try it out and trust him. By the end of the process he, and everyone else, was amazed at the honesty, the openness, the understanding, and the agreement that emerged from the dialogue. The following month, and for many months afterwards, the family requested, and used, the Group Dialogue to explore their ideas, thoughts, and feelings. Steve, hitherto the 'baby' of the family, suddenly became the sage and the facilitator.

Like all Inner Balancing steps, this one is simple and depends mainly on trusting that people have their own answers to their own questions. The power and synergy of the group is such that not only does the person presenting an issue gain from having others ask clarifying questions and respond to what they have understood, but that everyone else in the group benefits by connecting what they have heard with their own experience.

Consider any groups with which you are involved. What opportunity can you take to try a Group Dialogue? Jot down the groups that you already meet with or write the names of people whom you could invite to make up a group for this purpose. You will need between five and twelve people to make this work best. It helps to focus on the group of people who might take part in a Group Dialogue. This way you can relate each stage to the real people you know. ✐⬅📭

There are seven stages in the Group Dialogue, and there are some preparatory ones that are an important part of the process. The first part of the preparation is to have sufficient writing material on hand. Arrange the seating around a table or simply in a circle if this is preferred. Then establish a clear contract with the group. This means your saying what it is that you want to do, that you will be using a very clear structure consisting of seven stages, that you will facilitate the process and that everyone will be asked to participate. You will also want, in this contract, to note any concerns or questions people have. For example, you would need to satisfy people that if anything sensitive is discussed, it will remain confidential to the group.

The last part of the preparation is to invite everyone to think of an issue that they want to talk about in the group, specifying that this is something of their personal experience about which they have an unresolved question or concern, rather than a general or hypothetical issue. Ask each person to give this some thought, and allow about thirty seconds or a minute for this in silence. Then go around the group and ask each person if they have something that they would be prepared to talk about. If there is nobody, you can all go home, but in nearly twenty years and countless groups, I have never found this to happen. More likely, you will have at least three or four people prepared to share something, and you will need to select someone. You then have your initial presenter and you are ready for the first stage in the Group Dialogue.

Twelve people sat around a table, ready for their first Group Dialogue. This was a group of people who were on an Emotional Fitness course. We had been meeting for eight weeks, including two weekends, and had already used Listening Power, Learning from Experience, Lifescale and the Time Capsule. They were eager for more and a little intrigued that the table was there, since we usually sat around in a circle without a table.

Everyone said that they had an issue they could talk about, and four of the group indicated that they would be willing to do so. I invited Frank to be first, and said that the others would have an opportunity later during the evening, since we would break into two groups, and this would give a chance for up to four others to present, and other people to facilitate the process. This was their first demonstration, so I was facilitating this time around. I also said that we would be using a process of seven stages and that I would review this with them at the end. We already had a group learning contract, which had included agreements about confidentiality, respecting each other, being accountable for our actions and feelings, not interrupting and so on.

STAGE 1: PRESENTATION

I asked Frank to tell us what he wanted to say, and said that I would later be inviting others to ask him questions to help us all to understand anything that was not clear. This was what Frank said:

"I have been feeling quite stuck recently. I don't like the job I'm doing, and I know that I am working at something that is much too small for me. In fact I feel my whole life is too small. It's as though I have boxed myself in. Things are really busy at work and I have constant demands on my time. I'm in the kind of work where I have to react to other people when their computer goes down or they are having technical problems. It feels like I'm at everyone else's beck and call, and have no time to do what I love, which is being creative. Yesterday, my boss called me into his office and told me that another technical support worker had resigned, and that he didn't want to replace her. He wanted to share the work-

When your rage turns into tears, your soul is transforming.

load between me and the two others, which effectively meant asking me to take on a third extra work for no more pay."

I thanked Frank and gave a brief summary of what he had said, partly for him to hear, partly to give the other members of the group some time to consider their questions, and partly for Frank to see if he wanted to add or change anything. He did.

"I realize something hearing this," he said, "I always seem to get to the same place in my work after a couple of years or so. Then I change jobs a year or more after that and never get any further forward. I must have done that four or five times now over the past fifteen years."

I added this to my previous brief summary, then asked the group to ask Frank some questions that would help us and him to clarify what he was experiencing.

STAGE 2: CLARIFICATION

Just as in Listening Power, in order to understand what someone is really saying and more important, to enable the presenter to understand, we need to clarify what is being presented. This stage within the Group Dialogue is even more powerful, since we have the benefit of several people's perception and desire to understand. The value of this stage is that it avoids the double trap of the listeners making assumptions, therefore believing that we understand exactly what the presenter has said and jumping to the solutions in our own head from our own experience. In this case, it would be easy to do both of those things. After all, nothing Frank has said is very complicated or difficult to follow, and it appears that it would be easy to change this pattern and help Frank to get unstuck. But if that were true, how come Frank hasn't already done that? As we know, it's always easier to come up with plans to change other people's lives, than it is for ours. And don't we just love doing that!

Write down what questions you would ask Frank from his presentation so far.

Here are some of the questions people asked:

"You said you love being creative Frank. What do you do that's creative?"

"When you feel boxed in, and the work is too small for you, what do you mean?"

"How did you react to your boss? What would you like to change in the way you react?"

"You are aware of the pattern you get into in your work. Is this something that happens in any other areas of your life?"

These questions, and others, took Frank on a journey of some discovery. Here is some of what he said:

"I do love my creative side. But I don't do anything about it. I play the guitar, and it's one of the joys of my life; yet I haven't picked up my guitar for at least a year. Then I enjoy photography. I've taken some great shots in the mountains and by the ocean, and close-ups of plants and animals that are as good as anything you'll see in magazines. But they're all in boxes and I haven't taken my camera out since I don't know when. Even longer ago than my guitar. I tried some pottery last year and I was delighted with a couple of the things I made. But I stopped. So I'm not doing anything right now, and I don't know why.

"That feeling of being boxed in is strange, like I'm trapped and I don't know a way out. It feels claustrophobic; yes, too small. I'm like a rat in a cage. My life becomes boring and unfulfilled. People ask me to do things that I don't like. No, that's not true. I quite like doing the work; it's that I feel I have something, a lot, more to offer.

"When my boss told me he wanted me to do more, I felt resentful. I questioned him, and said that it was going to take longer to respond to some of the customers, but he said to do the best I could. I suppose I just said I'd do what I could. What I'd like to say is that I take a pride in doing things properly, and that I'd like to take on something more challenging. Instead of cutting back on staff, I believe it would have more value to the company and our customers to take on a couple more people. I would train them, and improve our customer service manual.

"This pattern I get into at work. I realize that it's not just work. There are many projects of my own that I have started and then dropped. It's happened with relationships too. It's like things always look good at the beginning, then I get bored, or maybe it's different from what I thought it would be like. I suppose even the things that I love, like playing the guitar, are part of the pattern. I wish I knew why. It feels like I don't deserve to have or to do the things I love."

Good intentions need wisdom to have good outcomes.

STAGE 3: GROUP SUMMARY

You will probably have noticed that the process of the Group Dialogue follows the same route as that of Listening Power. When working with people who have practiced Listening Power, it makes the Group Dialogue very easy. The facilitator needs to work harder to keep people on track when they are not familiar with Inner Balancing. It is also an excellent introduction to teams or groups in the workplace, since they experience a new, different and very powerful way of communicating.

The group summary is an example of how people begin to see things differently. While Listening Power gives the presenter the benefit of one person's summary, the Group Dialogue provides an opportunity to hear several people's perspective of what has been presented. The differences may often be very subtle, where people will pick up nuances and hear connections in a slightly different way. Sometimes, a listener in the group will have heard something or probably noticed a phrase or word that nobody else recognized as significant. The point of the group summary is that the presenter will hear those different versions and can decide which ones to accept, and which to reject. It is not a matter of being right or wrong. It is a matter of getting different and fuller perspectives.

Another thing about the summaries is that, as with Listening Power, this is not a memory test of all the details of what has been presented; it is an attempt by the listeners to put together the essence of what each has heard and understood.

It is the facilitator's job to point out these things to the group, and also to remind them that they are asked to notice not only what has been said, but also the body language, tone of voice, repeated words or phrases, and all the other signals and connections that come their way. The essence of what they will be asked to summarize will be the message and the story that those signals add up to.

Imagine you are one of the people listening to Frank in this Group Dialogue. You are at something of a disadvantage, since you have not been in the room with Frank, being able to see him, hear how he presents his story or have the full picture of what he has said. You do have enough to be able to make a summary of what you have read here, however, and it is good practice for you to write down that summary. Look back over the preceding paragraphs if you wish and complete this summary beginning with the words: 'I heard Frank say, I...' In other words, get into Frank's shoes, and write down the summary as though Frank is speaking.

This stage entails, first of all, each listener in the group writing down his or her own summary. When they have finished, the facilitator asks each one to read back what they have written, and for the presenter simply to listen and take in what is being said. The summaries, given as they are without any judgments or advice, are offered as gifts to the presenter. The facilitator tells the presenter to receive them in this way and to accept or reject whatever feels appropriate, again without judgment.

The facilitator does not make a summary unless there are only three other people in the group. Four is the smallest size group where this will work, twelve the biggest. In larger groups it is better to divide the group into two or more. The reason for the facilitator not making the summary is the tendency people have to see the facilitator as an 'expert', and that therefore his or her summary will be the 'right' one. Inner Balancing is about making each person the expert, and nobody more than anyone else. The facilitator is there to facilitate (make easy), not to take away others' abilities, even subtly, by stepping in with what may be seen as answers. The facilitator of Inner Balancing, including the Group Dialogue, is the Emotional Fitness Instructor, and an EFI understands that this role is an enabling and empowering one. All the facilitator has to do is to follow the processes and let the creativity happen.

Here are some of the summaries that were given back to Frank:

I heard Frank say, "I feel stuck in my work and in my life right now, and I see this as a pattern that I fall into. I don't understand why this is so. I know I'm creative, yet I can't seem to get up the energy to use my creative side."

I heard Frank say, "I feel trapped and boxed in. I have more to offer than I am currently using, and I wish I knew why. I get quite excited when I think about some ideas I have, yet I don't seem to be able to follow through, or I believe that someone or something else will block me."

I heard Frank say, "I thought I was just fed up with my current job, because my boss was asking too much of me. Now I realize that this is a pattern in my life, and that I don't let myself do what I love doing, even when nobody else is stopping me. I have some ideas about how I could do something more creative at work, and I have done some pottery, although I stopped. I also stopped playing my guitar and taking photographs. It feels as though I don't deserve to do what I like."

Only you can imprison your soul. Only you can free it.

I heard Frank say, "when I start out, I enjoy what I'm doing. Then I get bored and feel stuck and don't know how to get back my creativity. In work, the pattern is that I leave and start another job and go through the process again. Now I feel I'm in a box."

The listeners were able to observe the animated way in which Frank had talked about his ideas for work, and when he had shared his love for his artistic activities, in contrast to his dejected demeanour when talked about feeling stuck and 'in a box', hence some of the comments they made in their summaries.

STAGE 4: PRESENTER'S SUMMARY

Having heard the summaries from all the group members, the presenter is now asked to write down his or her own summary. While this is going on the rest of the group is doing nothing. This sometimes presents some discomfort. As the facilitator, it is helpful to observe what goes on here. In one group, a team of middle managers of a publishing company, they became quite agitated, wanting to check their messages or make a 'quick phone call', as though they had to be, and be seen to be, busy all the time. The irony was that the person who had been presenting had been talking about how much pressure she felt all the time, because of tight and often unrealistic deadlines. In discussing the process at the end of the Group Dialogue this was brought up and I was able to comment that the team had instantly reverted to their habitual 'crisis' mode, instead of recognizing what was going on and using the process to improve both their stress and their productivity. This discussion, added to the dialogue that had just taken place, provided them not only with insights into the problem, but also strategies that they could take to change that area of frustration into some positive, creative action. They established an improved method of internal communication and partnering that significantly reduced the editing and client response time, simply because far fewer errors were made due to misunderstandings at the beginning.

The 'doing nothing' time in the Group Dialogue has, inadvertently, become a positive time out or period of reflection. The facilitator can assist in this by suggesting that people think about their own summary and those of the others, and what it is that made up the differences. It is a time of potential learning, however new or experienced someone is with this process.

Meanwhile, back to Frank. Here is the summary he gave of his own experience, now with the benefit of the feedback he had received from eleven other people.

> *"I realize, for the first time, that I put myself into my own box. I now see that I never got any support from my family for being creative. The message I got was that I was a nuisance and just made a mess, or a noise, and that I should stop doing things I liked and get on with something more important. All of my toys and stuff were put into a big box and I had to keep them all there. Sometimes I'd climb in to save having to get them out and be shouted at. I hadn't recognized that I'm still doing that. So now I know why, and I know I want to change that."*

Much of this was a surprise to the rest of the group; it seemed a remarkable leap from where Frank had been, and apparently little to do with any of their summaries. Yet, it is the process of mirroring back, which is what the summary is, that allows the person to see what they would otherwise miss. Frank heard, first of all, that this was a pattern, second, that he didn't know why, third, that he put himself into a box, and fourth, that he loved creativity (play) and felt that he didn't deserve it. It was not all at remarkable, given this, for Frank to make his own connections, and come out with his new understanding and his own summary based on that. This was a wonderful example of the creative process that arises from simply listening, and the power of the Group Dialogue in allowing that to happen.

STAGE 5: ACTION FROM THE GROUP

Here, for some people, is an opportunity for them to give advice! At last, Inner Balancing seems to allow what many want to do naturally, despite all experience showing that advice seldom provides an opportunity for development, but rather for dependence. But wait! There is a distinction in the Group Dialogue between advice giving and empathetic suggestions for action, and the facilitator must make this distinction.

This stage in the Group Dialogue invites the listeners to put themselves into the skin of the presenter, having heard that person's summary. This means, as much as is possible, understanding and fully accepting who the presenter is and coming from his or her point of view and personality. This is different from 'if I were you', since it is patently obvious that I am not you, nor are you me. The question is more, 'as you, with what I now know about

Bombs beget bombs. Love begets love.

you, how do I believe you could best deal with this?'

Having heard (or in this case, read) Frank's own summary (not your own!), write down the action steps you would take as though you were Frank. Start your action points with 'as Frank, I will...' ↺⟸

When all the group members except for the presenter and facilitator have written out their action statements, they are invited to read them out. I always ask them to read only what they have written to prevent some from going into long explanations and justifications.

Here are a few of the statements made:

"As Frank, I will remember my box, and that I deserve to take all my toys out and play with them. I'll especially remember this when I talk with my boss (although I won't mention this at the time), and make my suggestions. At home, I will also remember my box and take out my guitar."

"As Frank, I will do one creative thing each day, even if it's for a short while. I will look at my job and see what things, in addition to what I already thought of, I could do to make it more creative and challenging. I'll stick a notice somewhere that says I can take everything out of my box if I want to."

"As Frank, I will tell my boss some of my ideas and tell him that I really want to help in making a difference. I will also ask him how he sees I could use more of my talents. If I get a negative response, I will look at how I can use my creativity in work that suits me."

"As Frank, I will get a box and use it to remind me that I want to jump out of it. When I feel I'm in the box, I will let myself do something I love. I will realize that, even if I feel boxed in at work, I have other things in my life that I can develop, whether they are creative activities or relationships, that make me feel good. When I feel stuck, I will ask someone from this group to help by listening."

Frank listened intently to all eleven statements. Some he asked to hear again. Sometimes he jotted down a note. He knew that he would be asked to make his own statement of action!

STAGE 6: ACTION FROM THE PRESENTER

That is, indeed, the next stage, together with another one for the rest of the group. While the presenter writes down his or her own action and the support that will be sought, the others are invited to write down the meaning and implications for them of what they have heard. Frank's action statement was this:

"I will remember my box. I have one, not the same one, that I keep at the foot of my bed. I have my photographs in there, most I took, but also old family ones. There is one of myself as a boy that I will mount and put on that box. When I start to feel boxed in, I'll think about that boy jumping out of the box. I am going to do at least one thing each day that inspires me, if not at work, somewhere else. I am going to talk with my boss tomorrow and give him my suggestions. I won't have expectations though, and if it's positive that's fine. If not, I will look at how else I can feel that I'm moving forward. And I'd like to invite you all over next Saturday to join me in a music and poetry evening."

This caused applause and delight from the group, and during the next five minutes people suggested what the evening could look like and that most of them would be able to come, bearing food and some creative contribution.

I asked Frank if he felt he would need any support in carrying out his action plan, and if so what that would be. After some more discussion about the now-developing concert party he said that he would call one or more of the group when he felt that he was not making the progress he wanted. "I know I need to review how I'm doing and I'd like your help." Several members of the group said that they would be happy to hear from him, and a couple said that they would make a point of asking how he was doing in a month.

STAGE 7: IMPLICATIONS AND PROCESS REVIEW

This last stage in the Group Dialogue is in two parts, the first of which might, depending on the circumstances, be dealt with in two ways. Where the group is made up of individuals who are together primarily for their own Emotional Fitness, the implications will focus on their individual experiences. Where the group is also connected in other ways, such a working team, or a family, or sports team, there will be implications for them to become more emotionally fit as a group, and usually this means taking some practical action steps as a group.

This part invites those who have been listeners to relate the issue to their own experience. In doing the Group Dialogue for over twenty years with hundreds of groups and thousands of people, I have never known anyone not to have seen a direct connection between the presenter's experience and their own.

Now you can really engage yourself with this particular Group Dialogue

Birth and death are certainties. It's the bit in between that's unclear.

and see where Frank's experience touches your own. Even if yours is entirely opposite to Frank's, this will be an opportunity for you to relate to being stuck, to feeling undeserving, to feeling in a box, or unfulfilled, or to being in a pattern that no longer serves you. There is a part of the question that refers to the process. This means the process of the Group Dialogue and how it has been experienced through the session. Your response will, necessarily, not be experiential in the way that it was for the members of this group. That will come later.

The question in stage 7 of the Group Dialogue is: 'what are the personal/professional implications for you of what the presenter has shared and from this process?' Answer that now from your experience. ◖◀▭

The Group Dialogue I have described here took place during an Emotional Fitness course, so met for the purposes of each person on it. The implications were therefore dealt with on an individual basis. People had already been asked to write down the implications and meanings for them, while Frank was writing down his action. Now I asked them to read out what they had written. Here are some samples of what was said:

"I realize that I don't use many of my talents and interests in my work, and that this stops me from enjoying my work as much as I could, and also means that I don't give as much as I could. I'm going to take a long look at how I behave. I'd like to sit down with Frank and check out how both of us are doing."

"This has shown me that I often feel stuck, or that I get in a rut at work, and how I am at home as well. I think I spend a lot of time at home not doing things that I enjoy, but feel like I am carrying out my duties. I used to love skating, and the closest I get now is taking my kids to hockey. I am going to get my skates out and see if the family want to come to the rink with me."

"At work, I'm the boss. This has made me stop and think how I probably overload some people and don't bring out the best in them. I'm going to do a Group Dialogue at our next managers' meeting and see what comes up."

"Listening to Frank reminded me that I haven't been hiking for over a year. I was in a hikers' group where I used to live, and I dropped it after I moved. I haven't looked for one here, and I'm sure there must be several."

"I was really struck by what Frank said about being discouraged from being creative. I wrote poetry when I was a kid, it just seemed to come naturally, but my parents ridiculed me, so I stopped. Now I have a hard time putting anything down in writing unless I'm asked to. I'm going to write something for Frank's

party and read it out. This will be hard for me – a real challenge – and I just ask for everybody's support."

The point of the Group Dialogue now becomes clear to everyone involved. It now moves from what might initially appear as a 'problem solving exercise' for one person, into something that becomes significant for everyone. Here, more than any other process within Inner Balancing, is the insight that each person's experience is both unique and universal. The emotionally fit person is able to see both, and as the listener, to separate his or her own experience while listening, then to make the connection between the other's experience and their own. As in Listening Power, the setting of a contract is crucial, and the seven-stage process of the Group Dialogue provides one.

When the group is one that meets together, say for work, the implications may include ones that affect the group as a whole. For example, in a group of teachers in an ESL school (English as a Second Language), one person presented an issue that had caused her students some confusion. While the Group Dialogue helped her to see how she would handle a similar situation more productively, it also led to the school improving its communication systems. In a large telecommunications corporation, a team of engineers developed a new project as a result of one person discussing the frustration he had felt from some dissatisfied customers. The company later calculated that it earned in excess of $8 million as a result of a one-hour Group Dialogue.

The second part of this final stage is for the group to review the process itself. This serves two purposes. One is to reinforce the learning that has taken place from what has been shared and discovered. The other is to remind the group of the seven stages of the Group Dialogue so that they can replicate the process.

Some comments in this part were:

"I found this very empowering. I didn't feel any pressure to come up with answers, and yet we all seemed to come up with something, not only for Frank, but for each one of us."

"What a powerful process. I'm going to use this in my Board meetings in future."

"I was amazed how well this worked. It's not like any meeting I've been in. The summaries and the action showed how well we all listened."

Laughing and crying are good for the soul. Try them both.

"This is the best part of Inner Balancing so far."

This last remark is quite a common one and shows, I think, not that the Group Dialogue is 'the best', but that by the time we use this process in a course people have become highly skilled listeners and are well attuned to the structured, yet freeing approach that Inner Balancing offers.

Now is the time for you to practice some Emotional Fitness training with a group. First, of course, you need to find a group. You need as few as three other people, beside yourself, or up to twelve. Six would be an excellent number to start with. Remember that if there are just four of you, you will need to include yourself in all the stages, including the summaries, action and implications. If there are more in the group, you may find it better not to include yourself in those stages.

In any case, you must set the scene, explain that you will be facilitating a seven-stage process and establish a contract with the group. Before you find a presenter, invite everyone to consider an issue (not necessarily a 'problem') that they may want to talk about in the group. Give them a couple of minutes to think about this. Then ask who has thought of something to share, and then ask who would be willing to do so. If you are doing this in a work team it is an ideal way to form an agenda, which you can write up on a flip chart or screen.

Invite the presenter to start by talking for about five minutes. It will be helpful for you to ask one or two clarifying questions before opening it out. This provides a model for others and allows you to steer people away from jumping in with their own experiences or suggestions. Don't, however, fall into the trap of getting so absorbed in the presenter's issue that you exclude the other members of the group. Your task is to conduct the process. Just as the conductor of an orchestra doesn't actually play the instruments, but inspires the musicians to play their best in harmony, you are there to enable the process to unfold, not to take it over. At the same time, and here is the delicate balance, you need to maintain an authority over the process. Once you allow people to deviate from the process, you will find that the discussion disintegrates into the normal, often sterile debate in which nobody learns and where the direction is steered by the person with the most persuasive voice. Your own learning will arise from practice. If you are not on an Emotional Fitness course, you will probably be doing this without the support of an Emotional Fitness Instructor. Expect to go through the Group Dialogue at least three times before feeling comfortable with it. I can guarantee you that you will learn more each time you facilitate the process.

Just to remind you, the seven stages of the Group Dialogue are:

Presentation
Clarification
Summaries from the group
Summary from the presenter
Action from the group
Action from the presenter
Implications and process review

We recreate our childhood until the child says "stop".

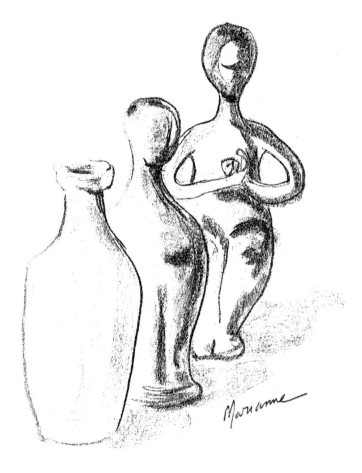

STEP 6: STORYTELLING

ONCE UPON A TIME…

Over 25 years ago, I sat on a train as it pulled out of a station in the small town in southeast England where I had been living. It was a misty, grey October day that is so typical of that part of the world. This was no typical day in my life. My suitcase was stuffed with most of my personal belongings. I was leaving my home for good after the breakdown of my first marriage of 15 years. I felt numb. Part of this was the sense of failure that I carried; mostly it was the intense grief I felt at leaving my children behind.

I kept questioning in my mind how I could possibly be doing this. Although I knew it to be right for me and my wife, if both of us wanted to feel more fulfilled, I could not reconcile my actions with my love for my daughters. My older daughter, then ten years old, had said to me days before, "Dad, don't stay together for us." Those words scorched themselves into my brain, while the silent tears of my younger daughter were like a fist grabbing at my heart.

As the train gathered pace and sped through the moist countryside of Kent, my mind raced with memories of my own childhood, trying somehow to make sense of what I was doing. I had always known that I had good recall of my early years. I found a notebook in my case and started to jot down a few words to remind me of some of those early events and experiences in my life. I wrote down six or seven, then another twelve, then more. The list grew beyond my imaginings, until I had written eighty or more words or brief phrases that reminded me of my childhood, all before the age of ten.

Something began to happen to me at that point. Here I was, consciously doing the hardest thing I had ever done in my life in leaving my children, and I was thinking and making notes on my own childhood. So much came flooding back to me. I gradually began to understand, in a clearer way than I ever had before, that the man I had become was connected to the boy I had been, in more ways than I had cared to see. Before the train had taken me to my temporary new destination, I started to write a story of my memory fragments.

Over the next few years, and many train journeys on my commutes to work, I completed the manuscript of what had become a book, consisting essentially of over 100 short stories, chronologically ordered, of a young boy's experience of life; all my personal and emotional recollections from before I was ten years old. I called it *Bender's Box,* since my great-grandfather featured prominently in the stories. He had an old metal box in which he kept his medals and other treasured items. His name was Isaac Bender, known to all as 'Daddy Bender'. I gave a copy to my father on his 70th birthday, and to my daughters, by then in their twenties.

When I came to Canada I sought ways of connecting with people, and discovered a writers' group meeting in a bookstore. I went along and was invited to return the following week, bringing something with me to read to the group. This was nerve-wracking. I had not originally intended my writings to be read by anyone else, other than my immediate family, and certainly had not envisioned myself reading to a group of practiced writers for critiquing.

The result was extraordinary. At first I received some positive and helpful feedback in terms of the writing. Then people began to relate some of their own personal childhood experiences. The rest of the evening was a sharing of these stories, until we had to call it to a halt when the owner of the bookstore wanted to close up. My initial reaction was of some dismay. I had wanted the feedback, and knew that others there had things to read. Then I realized that an important chord had been struck. On subsequent weeks, whenever I read from *Bender's Box,* the same thing happened. Later, I decided to run storytelling evenings, and then, because of the response, I included storytelling as one of the processes of Inner Balancing.

The Storytelling session begins with a little practice to get you in the mood, and also to ease you into the process.

Firstly, collect a few items from around the house. Maybe something like a pen, a vase, a flower, a candle. Perhaps you have a favourite object, or an unusual one, or one you just found. Collect about ten different things. Place all the items on a table, or on the floor. Then select one and pick it up. Take a good look at your object. Try to visualize yourself as the object. Let's say you have picked up a small rock that you once found on a beach. Imagine that you are the rock. What would it say? "I am a rock." Well, that's a start. Now you'd write down the story of the rock in its own words.

With the object that you have selected in front of you, take ten minutes to write down its story, as though you are the item. ✍

That was a warm-up exercise for you, and, if you did it, I hope you enjoyed it. Here now are a couple of excerpts from *Bender's Box,* after which you can write a story of your own.

No matter how much I wriggle or scream or drag my feet, the hands that hold mine keep pulling me forward down the middle of the road. Hedges on either side hide us from anyone who might come to rescue me. My insignificant hands are clutched too tightly, my puny arms are stretched too high over my head. On one side the hand grasping me belongs to Mummy, on the other side to Grandma.

Mummy's voice calls out gaily.

"Come along, let's swing."

They lift me off my feet in unison and I kick out against the indignity. It doesn't stop them; they start the singing.

"My Bonny lies over the ocean, my Bonny lies over the sea; my Bonny lies over the ocean; oh, bring back my Bonny to me."

And they swing me mercilessly as they chant.

"Bring back, bring back, oh, bring back my Bonny to me, to me; bring back, bring back, oh bring back my Bonny to me."

Other times I might enjoy this. Other times I might shriek with pleasure at the anticipation of the chorus, when I would be swept off my feet in a swirling arc. But not now. Today is different, and it's no good them pretending otherwise. I will fight against this outrage, struggle against their lightheartedness. They know I don't want to go back to the nursery school, and they especially know that I don't want to be left there alone. Perhaps they think I don't remember, or that I don't know where they are taking me.

Once before Mummy had taken me to the nursery school. It had seemed alright at first. There were lots of toys and a sand pit, and the lady showed me where to put my coat. She took me by the hand to talk to other children, which made me feel awkward, and I turned to find Mummy.

But she'd gone. Without any warning she had gone. Suddenly I was on my own with strange children and adults, not knowing why she had left me or if she would come back or if I would ever be home again. It was ages before she had returned for me and mopped up my tears and held me close.

Now they are trying to do the same to me again. I won't allow it. Tug down

One hug makes two people happy.

on one arm, now on the other, now both with all my might, now scream and stamp and drag my feet on the hard roadway.

I know we're going there. I knew as soon as we turned into this road. Whenever we go out it's almost always onto the Common, or occasionally just to the bottom of Park Street. Across the big road and down this lane has only meant the nursery school.

If I let my body go limp and scream more loudly they will give up and take me home. Grandma will pick me up and hold me close to her warm, bouncy body, and Mummy will take pity and kiss me and say she won't make me go. But the more I struggle, the tighter the grip on my hands and the more my arms are stretched until my armpits ache. Nothing will stop them dragging me to this place.

Whatever I do, they are taking absolutely no notice of me. They are chatting to each other over my head. I can even hear them, above the sound of my cries, laughing, shutting me out, giving me no attention. They don't care, and I'm too small to prevent us reaching the inevitable end of this journey. All I can do is wail as loudly as I can, let my shoes drag uncomfortably along the ground, and squirm hopelessly to try to wrench myself out of their ever-firmer grasp.

The nursery gates. I've lost the battle; I'm exhausted. In any case screaming in front of other people will be dangerous. Instead, I can do the low moaning, heaving of shoulders, drooping of head, sagging of body. We're in the school. I can see my shuffling feet stepping over the threshold, hear the noise of chattering children, feel my hand being passed over to another adult. A furtive glance upwards reveals the lady I saw last time. Long legs, flowery dress, fair hair, confident voice telling me, "we're going to have a lovely day today."

My feet have moved off into the garden. Quick peek sideways. Children are digging the ground with spades, watering the flowers with watering cans that spray drops in wide glistening circles, patting down earth with their hands.

"Now let's go inside and you can take off your coat. Do you remember where we hang it?"

This is the signal; one final effort. Hand up to my mouth, teeth biting side of finger, cry real tears.

"Don't worry, he'll be fine as soon as you go."

Head up, mouth open, eyes screwed up, scream. Through eyelashes I see Mummy and Grandma near the door. Mummy is wavering.

Look at feet again; my last chance. The moans are as mournful as I can get them, the shoulders as droopy as they will go, hands dangling uselessly in front of my knees.

"Bye-bye darling, have a lovely time; we'll be back soon; be a good boy."

Mummy's hand on my arm; pull it away. Out of the corner of my eye I see them walk through the door, out of the gate, and up the road.

The lady has her arms on my shoulders, and I am propelled back into the nursery school. Fists in eyes now, chest and shoulders heave.

"Look at this great big dolls' house. Are you going to say hello to the children?"

If I lower my fists very slightly I can just see over the top without them knowing. Slight, but firm pressure on my back shunts me onwards, across the polished wooden floor.

"Can you see all these toys? Which would you like to play with?"

This time I have to raise my fists slightly. It's more difficult, but I can make out the coloured wooden bricks and toy cars and dolls strewn about the floor. Deep, shaking breath, shudder of shoulders.

"What would you like to do?"

I let out a small moan. She pries one hand away from my eyes and takes it in hers. I leave it in there limply. She walks round the nursery, talks to children, sometimes kneels down, and drops my hand which flops loosely to my side, to help do up undone buttons or shoelaces, wipe noses, tie up ribbons.

"Would you like to go outside?"

I give a great sniff. She bends down and wipes my eyes and nose with the handkerchief that Mummy had stuffed into my pocket. Her eyes are blue, with long eyelashes that flicker over them as she carries out her task. She has a red spot on the end of her nose, and faint, feathery hair on her top lip and around her chin. She smells of milk and flowers. We go out into the garden. There are little squares of dark earth patched into the grass, and a longer strip of earth running along the side of the nursery wall. Red, yellow, and orange flowers are growing in some patches. Children are out here too, mostly running around on the grass but some are digging in the ground.

The lady takes me over to an empty patch where a small spade is standing straight up out of the earth.

"It would be lovely if you did some gardening."

The spade feels perfect in my hands.

Mummy's arrival is too soon and inconvenient. There are many more tasks to undertake. I've dug trenches with my spade, scattered seeds from a packet into

A secure border needs no barbed wire.

them, covered them up with earth, filled a red watering can, and sprayed water over the darkening soil so that the flowers will grow. Now I'm putting a plant into a flowerpot and have to fill it with more earth. Then I have to stay until my flowers come up as the lady had promised they would. When I explain this to Mummy, she and the lady laugh, and it's difficult to make them understand.

"He's been such a good boy; he's helped in the garden and worked very hard."

I take Mummy's hand to show her what I've done. She inspects my patch and can see where I've dug. She likes the spade, and especially the watering can when I demonstrate how the water comes out.

If I stay I can see the flowers come up; but if I go back home I can tell the others. I think I shall go back with Mummy now and come back tomorrow to see how my seeds have grown.

Remembering, then writing down the story, was a powerful enough experience for me. Reading it out to an audience brought me to another level of clarity and emotional understanding. Making sense of the connection between that story and my adult self gave me a deeper sense of who I am. There appeared to be three main lessons for me. I could use my Learning from Experience portfolio or a Time Capsule to discover more.

I had always, as long as I could remember, become edgy when parting, even for a short while, from somebody close to me. I would not want them to go or not want to leave them. I put this down to my feeling of abandonment when my mother died. Writing this story gave me another insight. I had felt abandoned much earlier, and it seemed to me I had never got rid of this feeling. I noticed my sense of disquiet next time my wife was leaving for the day, how I watched her until she was out of sight and wanted to be sure I knew when she would return. I used the Time Capsule to have a dialogue between my present adult and the child from this story at the point of his feeling abandoned. The image of me standing at the window waving to my wife until she turned the corner made me laugh, for I knew that the feeling was straight from that three-year-old who didn't want to be left alone, not from the man just happy to be waving to the woman he loved. As I gained this image, the feeling began to dissolve, and now seldom, if ever returns.

The second discovery was the connection between the small boy who felt so uncomfortable in the company of strangers, and the man who still does. The feeling is not simply being with new people, which I actually enjoy, but the sense of discomfort that I will have to explain myself, that they won't understand or even try to understand, who I am and what I want. My belief prior to writing this story was that this also stemmed from being shut down after my mother's death. Nobody would talk about her and she was constantly on my mind. I held this as a grudge for many years, until I realized that my father and other family members were doing the best they could and what they thought was right. With this second insight, I discovered that the root of my discomfort was much earlier. Now, in the company of strangers, which happens frequently, I call up the image of that little boy in me, still playing hard-to-get with somebody new. Then what I do is to turn the image around and see that others, too, are likely to be feeling a similar discomfort, and I open out my heart to them.

The third main lesson was my propensity to become completely absorbed in something that I enjoy doing, and how much that can lift my energy and spirit. After nearly sixty years, that remains, and, I hope will always be there. It is something I can value and celebrate in myself even more now that I can connect it with the small boy totally concentrating on his gardening, and with his vision of what it would become. The element of unreality still exists to a certain extent as well; I do want things to happen now, even though I understand they may take a long time to grow and blossom.

Here's another excerpt.

Daddy Bender's hand wraps itself right around mine. It's enormous and warm and comfortable and rough and rather hairy. It holds me not so tightly that it restrains me but just to show that we are companions.

We're on the Common; Daddy Bender and I. We know the Common very well. Just out of our door, past next-door where Aunty Sally and Jacky live, over the cattle-grid and here we are. The other way, down Park Street, to the big busy road, across to the nursery school and beyond is frightening and unknown. Here I'm grown-up and safe with Daddy Bender by my side. He knows everything and fears nothing.

We tramp across the vast expanse of grassland, trudging up the hills, dashing across into the dips until home is distant and out of sight.

"Look, there's our favourite place."

There in the direction of his pointing finger, I can see the great fallen-down tree trunk that we have discovered. I let go of his hand and run. The first bit leaves me gasping as I rush down into the dip and my legs judder up into my

Who would ever believe your true life story?

body. The second bit, up the gentle slope is easier but by the time I reach the tree trunk I'm breathless and it's hard to clamber up its side.

Reach up, foot on this lump sticking out, hold on to this other one, my body hugging the rough edges on the trunk, extract this arm trapped underneath me, haul myself over and I'm on the top. Just time to dangle my legs over the side as Daddy Bender catches me up, puffing out his cheeks, blowing out whistles of air. He lowers himself down onto the trunk and sits beside me, his feet firmly on the grass.

We sit there panting. His hand goes into his jacket pocket. What will it pull out this time? It's a small brown object looking like a tiny, pointed egg.

"See what I picked up. It's an acorn. Now I'll tell you something wonderful. If we plant this acorn it will grow into a big oak tree like that one over there. We're sitting on an old oak tree that has died and fallen over, so this tree trunk was once a tiny acorn like this."

The thing in the palm of his hand would turn into this tree trunk! I pick up the acorn while Daddy Bender talks on. I examine it between my fingers, squeeze it, turn it, stroke it, try to make it become a tree. He's talking about London now, as he often does.

"What's London?"

"It's a big town."

"What's a town?"

"Well, Hungerford is in the country and we came here because of the war. In the country we have the Common, with cows and sheep and the farm and the river and lots of trees and open space. A town is full of roads and houses and shops and cars and is much more crowded with people."

The old picture emerges; no, two pictures. One is quite clear, from my book. Lambs frolic about, a little girl wearing a long flowing dress; a border of flowers surrounds it all. This is the country. The town is harder to capture, this picture is not from a book; it's hazy and colourless and keeps fading from my mind. There is a wide road, cars, tiny people hurrying along, what seems like smoke. But I can't tell where the country ends and the town begins. I think it has something to do with the flowery border, because when I see the picture in my head, the lambs try to leap over the flowers into the grey smoke.

Daddy Bender is still talking.

"After the war we shall go back to London and you'll see what a town is."

"What's the war?"

Daddy Bender talks on but I can't get any pictures and it's boring, until he produces a coin from one of his secret pockets and shows me the King. Another pocket; his watch on a chain pressed close to my ear so I can hear its ticking. Back it goes. This time, between his fingers, a small white ball. I reach out; it disappears. It's not in this hand, nor that one. He pops it out of his ear, bounces it on the tree trunk, catches it, bounces it again and it sails away. I run to pick it up and we play with the ping-pong ball until, quite mysteriously, it gets lost and neither of us can find it.

"We shall have to go back home, it's getting close to tea-time."

We set off, exploring bushes on the way down to the fence where we wait until the train puffs its way along in the distance.

Back up the slope we have to go near the cows but I am hidden from them by Daddy Bender's legs. Now we reach the path and I can see the smoke rising from the cottage chimneys. It's hard to walk now; my legs and body feel heavy. Daddy Bender won't carry me, holds my hand tightly as we step gingerly across the cattle-grid.

The kitchen is warm and steamy and full of conversation and cooking.

My great-grandfather was to me the wisest and steadiest person in the world. He was the role model whom, unconsciously, I strived to become. There have been three other men in my life whom I have attached myself to and sought to emulate, and they all had echoes in some way, of Daddy Bender. The last of those men was Eugene Heimler. I needed no other after that, since I had discovered that the qualities I sought were already a part of me and I could use them positively and productively. The other day, a man whom I was counselling asked me how I had learned to do what I did. "You are so wise," he said to me. I suppose it did something to my ego to hear that, but I heard something much more meaningful to me. I heard that the boy on the Common had absorbed and finally integrated what he had learned from his Daddy Bender.

Now it's storytelling time for you. Often, after I have read out a couple of my stories to a group and then invited them to write one of their own, I hear the following objections. "I can't remember anything of my childhood," and "I can't write, I wouldn't know how to do it." These two excuses for resisting something that feels difficult or fearful are the most common. Probably you could find other more creative ones if you wanted to. I have never, in working with hundreds of people, found one who has not recalled something and been able to write it down. One woman claimed she remem-

Creativity is the singing of the soul.

bered nothing at all. I asked her to see what happened if she just jotted down some words. After ten minutes, when the others had written a story, she had come up with a list of over twenty words. I asked her to read out this list, and as she did so, her voice changed, her eyes opened wide and as she finished, she said, "there's a story in each one of these." She had done what I had done years before, recalled tiny fragments of her childhood that she had thought were gone. Every word brought up a memory for her and she realized that in each memory there was a story, and probably that she also had a book that could emerge from those stories. Apart from that incident, everyone else has, in ten minutes, written a story of wonder and personal significance. One man wrote a story about being eight years old when his father took him fishing. A wind blew up and caught the boy's new hat, sweeping it into the sea. He watched while his father cast his fishing line, trying to hook the hat. Three times he did this without success, then on the fourth attempt it worked and he managed to reel in the hat. The man who told this story related how he'd seen his dad as a great hero to do this. Then, his eyes filling up, he said, "It's my dad's birthday next month and I haven't known what to get him. I'm going to give him this story." That's what he did, and he told me later that he read the story in front of a large family gathering. "There wasn't a dry eye in the house," he said. And his father received the greatest gift he could have wished for.

Now, take ten minutes to write a story of your own. My suggestion is that you write it in the first person and the present tense to make it more immediate. Try to be there again and write from your own eyes and feelings, as though it is happening again. ✐◄▤

Look at your story and say what it means to you now. If you have the opportunity, read it to someone else and say what it means.

The mystery of your life lies within you, not in the stars.

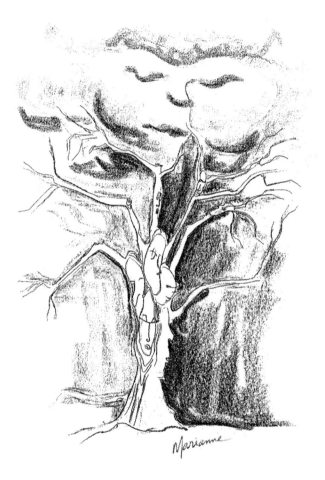

Marianne

# STEP 7: DREAMTIME

NOW I'M A TREE

*Shall my heart become
a tree heavy-laden with
fruit that I may gather
and give unto them?
And shall my desires flow
like a fountain that I
may fill their cups?
Am I a harp that the
hand of the mighty may
touch me, or a flute that
his breath may pass
through me?*

"The Prophet"
Kahlil Gibran (1883-1931)

Carl Jung was probably the father of modern dream interpretation, but it goes back a lot further than that. Sages, prophets and seers of all cultures, ancient and contemporary, have tried to make sense of the dreams that arise from our state of semi- or unconsciousness when we are asleep. What are our dreams trying to tell us?

Remember one of the first recordings of dream analysis? Joseph used to interpret his own dreams to his brothers who became so angry with him that they sold him as a slave. Later, having been thrown into jail in Egypt, he analyzed the dreams of two of his fellow prisoners. His reputation grew, and when Pharaoh heard of this he called for Joseph to tell him the meanings of the dreams that were troubling him. Pharaoh had dreamed of seven fat cows and seven thin ones; then seven plump sheaves of corn and seven stunted ones. The thins cows ate the fat ones, the sickly corn swallowed up the healthy. Joseph told Pharaoh that there would be seven years of plenty, followed by seven years of famine and that he'd better do something about it. You probably remember the rest. Suffice to say that Joseph saved the day, became reunited with his family, and everyone lived happily ever after, until other generations came along.

Jung's analysis was somewhat more scientific. In fact, following the footsteps of Sigmund Freud, Jung developed the understanding of the unconscious and the new human science of psychoanalysis to an extraordinary degree. His work paved the way to an awareness of the human mind that affects us deeply now. He became intensely interested in archetypes and symbols, which led him to explore fantasies and dreams. His thoughts on the 'collective unconscious' and on 'synchronicity' (it was he who coined the word), have given later generations much to consider.

Dreams were a tremendous fascination for him. In *Memories, Dreams and Reflections,* he writes:

Then, around Christmas of 1912, I had a dream. In the dream I found myself in a magnificent Italian loggia with pillars, a marble floor, and a marble balustrade. I was sitting on a gold Renaissance chair; in front of me was a table of rare beauty. It was made of green stone, like emerald. There I sat, looking out into the distance, for the loggia was set high upon the tower of a castle. My children were sitting at the table too.

Suddenly a white bird descended, a small sea gull or a dove. Gracefully, it came to rest on the table, and I signed to the children to be still so that they would not frighten away the pretty white bird. Immediately, the dove was transformed into a little girl, about eight years of age, with golden blond hair. She ran off with the children and played with them among the colonnades of the castle.

I remained lost in thought, musing about what I had just experienced. The little girl returned and tenderly placed her arms around my neck. Then she suddenly vanished; the dove was back and spoke slowly in a human voice. "Only in the first hours of the night can I transform myself into a human being, while the male dove is busy with the twelve dead." Then she flew off into the blue air, and I awoke.

I was greatly stirred. What business would a male dove be having with twelve dead people? In connection with the emerald table the story of the Tabula Smaragdina occurred to me, the emerald table in the alchemical legend of Hermes Trismegistos. He was said to have left behind him a table upon which the basic tenets of alchemical wisdom were engraved in Greek.

I also thought of the twelve apostles, the twelve months of the year, the signs of the zodiac etc. But I could find no solution to the enigma. Finally I had to give it up. All I knew with any certainty was that the dream indicated an unusual activation of the unconscious. But I knew no technique whereby I might get to the bottom of my inner process, and so there remained nothing for me to do but wait, go on with my life, and pay close attention to my fantasies.

From: Memories, Dream, Reflections by C. G. Jung

It sounds much more like the kind of dream that Jung would have than I would, or perhaps you. Jung did go on to explore and analyze dreams in terms of their 'universal meanings', so that certain images would relate to certain aspects of the unconscious mind. The work of dream analysis goes on today – quite a testament to someone who pioneered this work a century ago.

While Dreamtime in Inner Balancing has its source in the work of Jung, it discards the universality of symbols, and the analytic in favour of the individual, personal meanings of the dreamer. If Dr. Jung were with me today, I would ask him what the symbols in his dream mean to him, using more his emotional intelligence than his intellectual learning, for that is probably what tormented him in trying to understand. The work of Fritz Perls and the *gestalt* approach has, in this instance, much to offer, and that is the approach I have adapted for use in Inner Balancing. Here, the dreamer is in control of his or her own interpretation. As everywhere else in Inner Balancing, the belief is that we have all the understanding of ourselves within us. It is disempowering to put ourselves in the hands of an expert who will tell us who we are. Having somebody else interpret our dreams for us may be interesting and enlightening, but perhaps little more accurate than reading our daily horoscope, and certainly provides little opportunity for us to draw on our own inner wisdom.

I shall go through the Dreamtime process, but first you have to have a dream.

Perhaps you had a dream last night or very recently and it is still fresh in your mind. That would be perfect and you can begin working through the Dreamtime process. You might have an old, possibly recurring dream that you have often wondered about. That will be fine too. On the other hand, you may be one of those people who 'never dreams', which means that you do not remember your dreams. If this is the case, here are some things you can do to remedy your apparent dreamless state.

First, before you go to sleep, make a conscious choice to recall your dream when you wake up. Decide that you will dream, and make this the last thought you have as you close your eyes. (Of course this will lead to other thoughts, but you get the idea).

If you wake with the fragment of a dream in your mind, concentrate on it. Keep a notebook handy by your bed and jot down a word or two that will help remind you of your dream. If you don't want to disturb your sleeping partner, spend a few minutes thinking about the dream, and say to yourself

Do not ask "why the pain?" – ask "what may I do with it?"

what some of the symbols or events or people were.

First thing when you wake in the morning, recall your dream and write down some of the key fragments from it, if you haven't already done so.

You may have to try this several times before actually remembering either to do these things, or what your dream was. Use something that will remind you; a notice or picture that you will see as soon as you wake up; a piece of string tied around your finger; something more sophisticated, like a piece of micro-chip technology; anything that will be a memory jog immediately upon waking. As soon as you get the message, concentrate on recalling your dream. If it doesn't come in a few minutes, don't worry. Two things may happen. One is that you will recall nothing, in which case, just keep trying for a few nights over the coming week. Or, you may have a sudden, unexpected recollection of your dream later on during the day. Some of my clearest dream memories appear when I am having a shower, or when somebody says something that triggers what I dreamt the night before. The trick here is to make a note, even a very brief one, immediately. Once you have recalled your dream, and have a word or an image or two that reminds you of it, try drawing some of the images on a sketchpad. This will give you a fuller picture for when you come to work on the dream.

The more you practice this, the more you are likely to recall your dreams on a regular basis, and begin to enjoy them in a way that may not have seemed possible before. Then, once you do recall your dreams, you can use the Dreamtime process to have your dreams talk to you in a new and enlightening way.

The Dreamtime process goes like this:

1. Take a large sheet of paper (an ideal size is the sheet that comes with a flip chart, or a poster size. Using some coloured marker pens, draw a fragment of your dream. If it was a long, complicated dream, choose which part of it you want to focus on and draw this. If you don't believe you can draw, try it anyway. Use colours as close to what your dream experience tells you to use.

2. When you are satisfied that you have illustrated your dream experience, or at least that fragment of it that you wish to explore right now, take a look at each of the images you have created, and write the words they are saying. You do this in the same way as cartoon characters speak, when the words they say (or think) appear in bubbles out of their head. The images do not need to be people, just imagine that each thing you have drawn has sufficient value to have something to say. For example, if

you have drawn a tree that is shedding its leaves, start with just that. You might write, "I am a tree. My leaves are shedding, and I can't stop that, because it's autumn. My branches are showing through. I am sorry to lose my leaves, although they are withered and brown. My branches are sturdy and will make it through winter, ready to grow new leaves." If you have drawn a boy climbing up the tree, you might say something like, "I am a small boy. I want to get to the top of this tree and hide in the branches, but when the leaves fall I can be seen. I must keep climbing to the top and get there before the leaves all disappear." Of course, you would write these things if your dream were telling you that this was so. If you have no notion of what the boy was doing, you could merely write: "I am a small boy climbing a tree." The chances are fairly high, however, that if you concentrate on your dream, you will discover more about the tree and the boy, and what they are saying or thinking. Remember always to start your quote with "I", so that each symbol or person is talking from the first person and the present tense. Often, you will be in the dream, so it is more obvious that you will write it that way, but use the same approach for all of the images.

3. After you have written quotes for all of the images in your dream, including multiple images (perhaps the same boy is depicted several times doing different things, for example), and for the images that appear incidental to you (the sky, the sun, the grass, a cloud etc.), put them into a sequence as close as possible to the sequence in your dream, so that you have a story emerging. Number them on the sheet in this sequence.

4. Now say out loud what you have written, in sequence, exactly as you have written it. The ideal is to read this out to a group engaged in an Emotional Fitness course or at least to a group you can trust well enough to take part in this Dreamtime process. Failing that, invite a trusted friend to listen to you. As a last resort, simply say it out loud, recording yourself on an audiotape.

5. The next phase is to hear back what you have said. Depending on your circumstance, you will hear this from the group, or on tape. If you are in a group, allocate a different role, or 'voice' to each of the people there, so that the first voice is one person, the second another, and so on. You may have to ask people to double up, as long as they know which voice or

Once you've lived a little, why not go the whole way?

voices they have, and where they are in the sequence. Listen carefully to what you are hearing back.

6. Next, having heard everyone or your own voice repeating the words, all starting with 'I', imagine that each symbol really is you. So, instead of the tree saying, "I am a tree. My leaves are shedding and I can't stop that because it's autumn. My branches are showing through. I am sorry to lose my leaves, although they are withered and brown. My branches are sturdy and will make it through winter, ready to grow new leaves," say, "my leaves are shedding and I can't stop that, because it's autumn. My branches are showing through. I am sorry to lose my leaves, although they are withered and brown. My branches are sturdy and will make it through winter, ready to grow new leaves," and ask yourself, "what does that mean to me?" The answer may be something like, "I feel as though I'm losing some of my old habits as I'm getting older. This exposes me a bit and although it feels a little scary, I know that I'm strong enough to handle the change and can look forward to new things in my life." Or, as the boy, saying, "I am a small boy. I want to get to the top of this tree and hide in the branches, but when the leaves fall I can be seen. I must keep climbing to the top and get there before the leaves all disappear," your meaning may be, "I want to hide and, at the same time, keep moving up. It feels like I am very inexperienced and in a hurry to grow."

7. Once you have a clearer understanding of what your dream is telling you, or more accurately, what your unconscious mind is saying, you can begin to choose how to react. Joseph's interpretation of Pharaoh's dream, and his subsequent recommendations, helped Pharaoh to build a storehouse of corn so that when a famine arrived the Egyptians were ready for it. In your case, you might want to look at some options. Firstly, look at what you may want to change in the picture you now have of yourself. In our example, of the tree and the small boy, the dreamer might want to gain more experience and confidence and instead of hiding, learn to connect more with others. In this case, the dreamer will ask the group to say different things. The person playing the role of the tree might be asked to say, "I am proud of my branches and I am looking forward to growing my new leaves." The small boy might say, "I love climbing the tree. I feel powerful when I'm up here and I can see everything. This is good experience for me."

8. Have the group members say the words that the dreamer gives them. With a group you can conduct it as though it were the scene from a play,

with you, the dreamer, as the audience and the director.

9. Finally, the dreamer makes a summary of all that he or she has experienced from sharing this dream and chooses what, if any, course of action to take. In the example we have used, the dreamer may now see the message as, "I'm proud of my experience and what I have to offer, and I'm looking forward to trying out new things. I'm going to get a clearer view of possibilities for myself. When I do that, I feel quite powerful and can enjoy being inexperienced at something new, because I know what I bring."

If problems are opportunities, how unlucky you are to have missed some.

STEP 8: THE MIRROR
ME THROUGH THE LOOKING GLASS

What lies behind us, and what lies before us, are tiny matters compared to what lies within us.

Ralph Waldo Emerson
(1803-1882)

The whole of the Inner Balancing process describes ways of looking at ourselves through eyes that become increasingly clearer. Listening Power enables us to be heard in a way that mirrors back to us what we are thinking and feeling, by the listener acting as the reflector so that we get to hear and understand ourselves in ways that help us to make sense of who we are and what we want, and then to make the decisions and take the actions that help us to move forward in the direction that we want and need to take in life. Listening to others in this way enhances our relationships with them in a way that no other could.

The Mirror is the step in Inner Balancing that literally does face us with ourselves.

This is not an easy thing to do. Some preparation is needed, together with a comfortable and safe environment. As with all the other processes, this is most effective when carried out in a group setting with others taking an Emotional Fitness course, or at least with a mentor able to hear and encourage you.

I don't know about you, but I look in the mirror first thing in the morning when I'm in the bathroom. My main reason is to make sure I'm shaving properly or that my hair is in reasonable order. Sometimes I catch myself seeing my reflection in the mirror of an elevator or in a store window, self-consciously and bizarrely checking that I am who I'm supposed to be. What I see in those moments are the superficial images of myself that give me a limited two-dimensional view of a particular aspect of what others may see. When I peer more closely, gazing into my eyes, I begin to see something else. I begin to reach deeper into myself, to touch the edges of my soul. Who am I at that moment as I become more conscious of the person behind the reflection?

My first experience of delving into the deeper part of my being through the use of a mirror was on a weekend course that I attended over 30 years ago. I was unprepared, as, I believe, were many of the others present. While it was a profound and exhilarating experience, the groundwork had not been sufficient to support me in the questions that it brought up in me. When, years later, on an Emotional Fitness course, another facilitator suggested using a mirror, I was hesitant at first, then realized that people had already been through all the other Inner Balancing steps. I recognized that I needed to put aside my own experience, because this was bound to be different, given the different circumstances. That first time we tried, it changed my perspective completely. Two of the people who were at that session left an impact on me that I shall never forget.

Lin was a lively, sensitive, highly intelligent, passionate woman. She was a human resources consultant, and had become excited with some of the ideas she had been getting to develop her work. She was the first to pick up the mirror that lay on the table in the centre of the circle. She looked into it, touched her blonde hair self-consciously, then slowly ran her fingers along the contours of her face. It was as though she had never seen herself before. She was silent for a long time. Her first words, said in a tone of surprise, even in awe, were, "you are beautiful."

I knew some of Lin's story. She had witnessed serious physical abuse in her family, and had herself been a victim of it. As a child she had seldom received any positive messages about herself. She looked deep into the mirror close to her face, stroked the faint shadows and fainter lines under her eyes, and spoke to her reflection in an almost inaudible whisper. "And you are beautiful inside. You have been on such a journey in your life and you have learned a lot. Now that I can really see you, I know how much beauty and how much love you have to offer." She gazed even more deeply, searching, it seemed, to reach into her soul. "Ah," she said, "now I can find you. You have been hiding for a long time and I want you to come out. I want to show you it's safe now. We have a great deal to do together, you and I. I'm the one who has been getting on with life, ignoring my real feelings and hopes, and ignoring who I really am inside. I won't ignore you any more. Now I can be authentically me. I love you." And Lin began to cry gently, smiling through her tears at the person she was seeing, it seems, for the first time. She looked radiant as she put the mirror back in its place. Her main reason for coming onto the course had been to become authentic.

A little later the same day, Carol decided to take her turn. It was not the first time that Carol had looked into this mirror. It was hers, and she given it to me for us to use specifically for this purpose. After I had told the group that we would be using a mirror she had insisted on bringing this one, since it had particular memories for her. We are using the same mirror to this day.

Carol had been dealing with a number of physical illnesses over a long period. On top of that, she had been seriously injured in a car accident, and was slowly recovering. The smile that came over Carol's face as she stared into the mirror was beatific. "Oooh", she said, as she watched herself emerge. She too looked deeply and at length without saying much, peering into the mirror as her face became relaxed, peaceful and somehow angelic. "Oooh," she murmured again, "I love the way I'm looking. It feels good, just to see who's there, and looking so happy and healthy; just getting beyond what's in front. There is more and more of me all the time, knowing that now is the time to be living life and enjoying being me." Carol took her eyes off the mirror for a moment and scanned the room, smiling at each person in turn, then brought her attention back to her own reflection. "See how when you smile, everyone does that back to you. You even do it to yourself, and the world feels peaceful."

Lin and Carol are no longer with us. Lin died tragically and suddenly; Carol about two years later. Both of them were at peace as they saw themselves fully in the mirror, excited with life and delighted with who they were. I believe they kept that with them. Both of them certainly touched me and many, many others deeply. I cannot hold this mirror up without thinking of them and seeing their images smiling back at me. I miss them, but I know they are always here.

When I look into the mirror myself I see me, and within me, I see my great-grandfather, my grandmother and my mother. They each brought qualities to me that remain with me. They have always been there, even through the thirty years when I believed that I had lost them. Now I know that my strength comes from my great-grandfather, my gentleness from my grandmother, my smile from my mother. As I look longer and further into the

Every child's birthright is to know the love of its mother and father.

mirror, I see my daughters and grandsons, and the qualities they have inherited and will pass on. If that's not love that I see when I now hold the mirror up to myself, I don't know what is. I guess that when I first used the mirror all those years ago, I was still not able to see them, and therefore those qualities, in me. Maybe I got a glimpse and didn't know what I was seeing, or what to do with it.

To try The Mirror out for yourself, make sure you have a good-sized hand mirror, one that you can hold up comfortably that is big enough for you to see your whole face in. Then get yourself in a relaxed mood. You will be holding up the mirror for about ten minutes. You need to be sitting, and certain that you won't be disturbed. You can do this in a group, which is preferable, or with one other person, or simply on your own.

When you are ready hold up the mirror in front of your face, so that you can see only yourself. Spend a little time just looking. Notice everything about your face and its features. What do you like or not like? Now begin to talk to yourself in the mirror, always keeping your eyes on yourself. If you feel distracted by something or other people being there, draw yourself back to your reflection. This is the person you are talking to and receiving from.

Look more deeply as you talk, or give yourself some silent time if you wish. You have at least ten minutes. If you can think of nothing to say after a minute, you still have nine more minutes. Keep concentrating on yourself in the mirror. Have a conversation. Who do you see? How do you feel about this person? What is going on inside this person? What do want to confide? Is there something you want to ask or to offer? What is going on behind those eyes?

In a group or with another person, if you have an agreement that they may do so, someone else may ask you a question. If this happens, keep looking in the mirror, not at the person who asked the question. Imagine that the question comes through the mirror. You may take longer than ten minutes if you wish, especially if others are asking questions, but don't take less. When you are finished or the time is up, put down the mirror.

Spend a little time in silence, alone or in the group. Then talk about this experience and what it meant to you.

When you have done that, write down what happened and how it felt, or whatever you want to record. ✐

To be fully appreciated, The Mirror should be used once you have gone through the other Inner Balancing steps and in the company of others who have experienced the same. My experience of facing myself in The Mirror is that it is different every time, that I see something that I may not have seen before (apart from extra lines), and that I get to appreciate myself more. It is also always a surprise, always a 'first time', as I hold the mirror up. It's not at all like shaving!

The more you use The Mirror, the more you may begin to notice others in a different light as well. Imagine looking into someone's eyes the way you looked into your own. It would be pretty uncomfortable to do this with an acquaintance or business associate, and you might find yourself in trouble in our society if you did. When you look into your sweetheart's eyes, or your child's, you know the intimacy that this engenders.

You don't need to search into someone's eyes with such intensity, however, to get to connect with them in a deeper way. The notion that there is 'someone else' in there, someone who has thoughts and feelings more profound than they might ever say to you, that they, in many ways, are just like you, may give you a much greater appreciation of that person. Simply having had the experience of The Mirror for yourself, and imagining that other person doing the same thing, can have a significant affect on how you see them, and therefore interact with them.

When Doug used The Mirror, he had a hard time at first seeing or saying anything positive about himself. After less than a minute he wanted to put it down and stop the process. I encouraged him to stick with it, telling him that he need not feel he had to say anything, simply look into the mirror. His eyes wandered outside the glass at first, then he seemed to relax (or surrender) and spent about three minutes just looking into his reflection. "You're not so bad, you know," he muttered. "You think you're a fraud, but you're really a good guy. The trouble is, you've had to put out a different image to succeed; then you think you don't deserve that success. The truth is, you've really worked hard to deserve it. It just doesn't come naturally, and now I see that you have never needed to put that other image out. You could just be you. It's only you that has cared about looking the part, being the kind of boss who has to know and control everything, when I now understand that it's been my fear of failure that has made me hang on. Underneath, I know that I want, you want I mean, to have fun, and trust that everything will work fine. Everyone else around me is perfectly capable of doing what they do, and most of them wouldn't care if I relaxed more and didn't get so involved in everything. In fact, they'd probably be delighted. So why don't you

Just think what God could have done with an eighth day.

just do that my friend. You deserve a break, and you can give everyone else a break at the same time, and just let them do what they do best, their own job."

The following week, Doug reported that something strange had happened. "When I was at work, I looked at everyone differently. I saw them in my mind looking into a mirror and discovering something positive about themselves, and I saw them in very different ways. When I started saying to people that I'd be taking more of a back seat, and telling them how well I thought they were doing, they looked at me, kind of funny at first. Then, one by one, over the next few days, they came up to me and asked me for help with something, or told me that it was time I relaxed a little. A few seemed worried about me, wondered if I was OK, or if I was going to sell the business. They all wanted to support me, or show how they valued me in some way. It's never happened before. We seem to know each other better. When we had our monthly update meeting yesterday, there was a different, much more co-operative atmosphere. We agreed more action than we usually do in three meetings. And I finished up with far less to do at the end."

One couple who were on a course together and did The Mirror, found that they each heard more about the other than they had previously in ten years of marriage, even with sharing the Time Capsule and other processes. They decided to try it at home afterwards, and reported that they then practiced looking at each other without The Mirror, saying what they now saw in and behind the other's eyes. They told me that the level of intimacy and understanding they found was deeper than anything they had experienced. "We truly touched each other's souls," they said.

If you believe, as the saying goes, 'the eyes are the windows to the soul', or as the French say *'les yeux sont le miroir de l'âme'*, then you will understand what happens when you gaze through The Mirror into your own eyes, or into the eyes of someone else. When you experience it, you will know for sure.

$$m + pb + e = s$$

STEP 9: CONNECTIONS

PULL MYSELF TOGETHER

My hope is that by the time you get to this page you will have travelled further along your journey of self-discovery and Emotional Fitness, just as I indicated at the start. Your part in this will have been to have fully experienced the Inner Balancing steps along the way. Now we are moving towards the last of these steps, although of course not the end of your journey.

I call this last step Connections, which is a way for you to pull together much of what you have been doing. During Connections, you will also be able to combine some or all of the rest of Inner Balancing. Listening Power will certainly be there, for without it, there will be little opportunity to grow. You may notice elements of Learning from Experience and some of the questions in the Lifescale, as well as the Time Capsule and Group Dialogue. Storytelling will be strong, and even Dreamtime may creep in.

Like all the rest of Inner Balancing, Connections has a simple format with powerful results. There are three stages in this process of Connections. The first is the connection between you and a symbol or item of significance that you can relate to. The second stage is the connection you now have with the contract that you established with yourself at the beginning of your Emotional Fitness journey. The third stage is the connection that you have made with others, through giving and receiving acknowledgements.

Let me take you through the first stage with an example of what happened the first time I used it in a group, with me as the guinea pig. While it works the best within a group, it is also something that two people can do together.

Each person brings along to the group an item of significance to them. This might be something they have owned for many years, or have more recently acquired. It may be a photograph or painting, a piece of pottery or artifact, a book or letter; anything as long as it has a personal meaning to the individual bringing it. One person brought an old shoe, another a guitar.

The first time I did this I brought a gold sovereign, an old English coin in currency before the British pound note was circulated and placed it, along with all the other items, in the middle of the circle of people. Since the objects that people bring are all precious to them and in fact represent an important part of who they are, the space that is made for them needs to be given special attention. I usually provide a rug, perhaps with a candle as a centrepiece, just big enough to make sure that everyone can easily place their item on it. It doesn't always work, as when somebody brought along a large painting that she had done several years before. We had to prop that up against the wall, otherwise it would have taken up all the space.

The first person volunteers to pick up his or her own item and to talk about it, its meaning to them, and the personal story that they attach to it. The rest of the group can ask questions. When this is done at the end of an Emotional Fitness course, the story is often of the personal learning journey that the individual has taken, using their item as a reference.

After the first person has finished, he or she selects an item, and the owner of that takes their turn next.

When, after about the fifth person to go, my item was selected, I picked up my sovereign. Nobody in the room knew what it was, so I explained that it was a real gold sovereign, made in the time of Queen Victoria, and used as currency in England up until the early part of the twentieth century, until the pound note took over. Mine was dated 1885. I held the coin in between my thumb and forefinger, feeling a strange mixture of joy and sorrow, as though I was both finding and losing something at the same time. My emotions were intense, and I noticed that my heart was beating faster, and my throat was a little choked, making my voice sound husky.

"This belonged to my great-grandfather, whom everyone in the family called Daddy Bender," I started. "He died when I was seven. I recall him showing me this sovereign, along with various medals and other treasured items that he kept in a metal box that he had made. After he died, I never saw it again, at least not until fairly recently. But I had his box when I was eighteen, when my father took me to the bank to collect my inheritance. There turned out to be nothing in the box, except for a few pieces of paper that his daughter, my grandmother, had obviously put in there. One was a brief love letter to her from my grandfather.

Another was my mother's death certificate. Those things, and the box itself, were all the inheritance I could have wished for, even at eighteen, although I wondered where the medals and the sovereign had disappeared to. About 35 years later, when I moved to France for a short while to start a new phase in my life, I decided to investigate the box. I heard something rattling inside the metal lining, and pried it open. Out fell a gold collar-stud and this sovereign, which I recognized immediately, because it has a tiny clasp welded onto its edge so that Daddy Bender could attach it to his medal ribbon."

I paused, and somebody asked me; "What does it mean to you to have it now?"

"This is one of the few tangible links with him that I have," I said. "I realize how much he meant to me. Even though he died so long ago, I know that he was the man who influenced me most in my life. I feel his strength in me, and his compassion. Occasionally, when somebody tells me that I have said something wise, I feel his words coming through me, although I remember hardly anything he said. I do remember the sense of wisdom that I felt from him. In a way, he has always been my mentor. I found a few others in my life, including John Heimler, whom I saw as my guide, but I know that Daddy Bender has always been there for me. So, this sovereign means to me the link between my wise, strong and compassionate guide and who I am today, which is trying to be those things for myself and others. I feel tremendous warmth coming from this sovereign. I think I was about 40 when I cried for the first time at the loss of my great-grandfather, and that was also the first time that I said out loud, although I was alone in my car listening to a tape that had triggered my emotion, "I love you, Daddy Bender". That's what I feel from this sovereign; his love coming through me, and my love for him, and my love for the love I have in me. It's the discovery that I never lost that love just because he, and my mother and my grandmother all died within a couple of years. The love remains as long as I allow myself to have it within me."

Within the Connections session, several of those who shared their stories, including me, went into a Time Capsule. My own involved my talking to my six-year old self when I was looking at the sovereign held in Daddy Bender's hand. It was a powerful and moving experience for me, and allowed me to tell myself that this sovereign, this moment, and love itself, would never be lost, only mislaid for a while, until I was ready to reclaim it.

When I had finished, I put down the sovereign and waited for the next phase – feedback from the others.

Great wealth is no substitute for richness of the soul.

This stage in the process of Connections is the stage of acknowledgement. Each member of the group offers their gift. It is their insight into the person who has just shared, their understanding of what they have received from the person. In my case I heard a lot about how the qualities that I had described in my great-grandfather shined through in me, and how I had affected their lives in one way or another, that they were grateful for what they had gained from me, and now that they understood, that they were grateful for Daddy Bender.

I had known of the importance of the sovereign. I had never before put it into words or understood its real meaning to me, until I spoke it out loud. Since then, I feel closer to Daddy Bender, which means feeling closer to those qualities that I received from him. I believe that has made me a better person. No longer am I attempting to fill his shoes, and feeling too small for them. Now I have accepted my own greatness. One day that sovereign will go to one of my own grandsons, and, who knows, to my great-grandchild.

These were all valuable insights and connections for me. I made another connection some time later. My great-grandfather's first name was Isaac, and I recalled seeing his initials IB on a hammer that he used in his many carpentry projects. And IB is also Inner Balancing.

But the most important connection I made was also the most important discovery leading to a leap forward in my own life.

Once I truly understood and accepted my own qualities I was able to take a major step to bring Emotional Fitness to others. No longer was it good enough to wait for people to come to me and to teach Inner Balancing to a few. I became ready to offer it to a far wider audience and to teach others who would become Emotional Fitness Instructors, taking Inner Balancing out to thousands instead of hundreds.

The acknowledgement stage is an extraordinary experience, quite literally, for it is so rare to give and receive open and honest feedback in an environment of trust that it may never happen for most people. Within a group that has spent one hundred hours of intense personal exploration, an understanding is reached that is seldom experienced even in the closest relationships. The opportunity to hear what others have experienced of you in such a setting is not only rare, therefore, it is also moving and highly rewarding. It is a sharing of gifts at the highest level.

The third stage in Connections is the review of your personal Emotional Fitness learning contract. You may have taken the opportunity to review it as you have been proceeding. This is the time to connect yourself then with yourself now. What have you noticed about yourself? How are you feeling about yourself? What questions do you have now?

Do you recall the personal Emotional Fitness learning contracts of Maureen, Jim, Claudette and Greg, way back in the introduction? Here they are again:

Maureen: I want to learn to be myself. I want to discover my purpose and to find a way of expressing myself in my work that is more meaningful to me.

Jim: I want to improve my relationships, with my wife and children, and especially with myself. I want to learn to listen more.

Claudette: I need to create more peace in my life. I don't want to have to feel in control all the time. I'd like to reach a state of wisdom.

Greg: I want to deal with my feelings of guilt, and change some of my negative self-beliefs into positive ones. I want to listen to myself more and not just follow other people's expectations of me.

All four of them reviewed their contracts at the end of their Emotional Fitness course. Here is what they said:

Maureen: I have realized that I have been holding back from doing what I have secretly wanted to do for years. I have already registered for the training course I need to take in order to pursue my chosen profession. I have acknowledged that I have a natural talent for the healing arts, and that's what I will be doing. I have never felt so free, or so enthusiastic about anything in my life.

Jim: It feels like the blinders have been taken off. I have to admit that I was scared and quite honestly didn't believe that anything would change; mainly because I thought everyone else had to change. Just learning how to listen has improved my relationships beyond belief. I have taken this into my life.

Claudette: I have to laugh when I look at my contract now. I had wisdom all along, and didn't know it because I felt that I had too many doubts. I worried about those doubts, which made me anxious. Now I can just smile at them, because I understand that the doubts are the source of my wisdom.

Greg: I notice that I still have some feelings of guilt. But now, I know who is feeling guilty – my little child – and I can reassure him. For me, it's no longer about

Spirituality unifies humanity. Religion divides humanity.

not feeling negative, it's about how I can connect with that small Greg who needs my support. Then I find that he rewards me with his deeper happiness and innocent wisdom. Spooky, but it works for me. I feel the happiest I have ever felt, and it rubs off on the people around me.

Find an item that is significant to you. Go through the process of Connections described above, or if you are not in a group meet with a mentor who will listen to you talk about it, its story, and its meaning and connections to you. Receive and give acknowledgment in terms of open, honest feedback. Review your contract. Write down your connections.

Here is my acknowledgement to you. I thank you for the time you have taken, not just to read this book, but also to have entered into its spirit. The distance in time and space between me writing this, and your reading it, is suddenly narrowed. Whoever you are, it feels to me that you are in my consciousness right now. As you read this, I could be anywhere. The important thing is that you are here, you are present with yourself in your own consciousness, and you have shown, by having arrived at this page, a desire and a capacity for personal growth and understanding that in itself demonstrates Emotional Fitness.

Don't be a back seat driver in your own life.

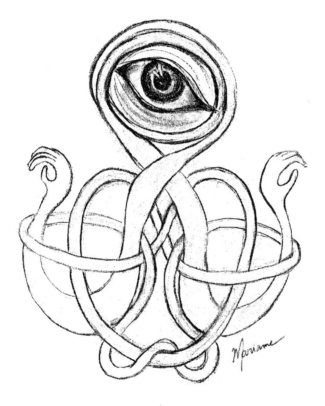

CONCLUSION

NOW I'M OUT. WHERE DO I GO?

If you have decided that you would like to take Emotional Fitness to others as well as yourself, this chapter is for you.

I have been teaching Emotional Fitness since 1986 when I began to run courses using the best processes I had learned from a variety of wonderful pioneers. I didn't know I was offering Emotional Fitness, nor did I understand that this was the beginning of Inner Balancing. My students taught me that. Over the years, in running courses from one weekend to six months in duration, I discovered Inner Balancing; or perhaps it discovered me. It and I was there, waiting to be found. All I had to do was listen and make sense of what I heard, and respond in a healthy way to it, which is what Emotional Fitness is all about.

Recently I had the incredible experience of taking an Emotional Fitness course taught by two people whom I had trained. As a bonus my wife took part in the same course, so that we could participate equally. Was there more for me to learn? You bet there was! In the first few sessions I made some important discoveries about myself. I took a hard look at what sometimes held me back from creating what I wanted, and that shot me straight back into my core life themes: disconnecting with others because 'they may leave and are not to be trusted', and not trusting myself because 'my thoughts and beliefs are not accepted by others'. Old stuff, and not significant enough now to have much impact on me most of the time. Yet those internal stories I give myself are so deeply ingrained that they emerge whenever I am challenged outside of my comfort zones. The action I am taking is to trust others more by sharing myself including the manuscripts of this book, with others around me and to 'come out' by speaking and making presentations to more groups and organizations outside my closer networks. Almost immediately after having taken that decision I began to be invited to speak about Emotional Fitness to entrepreneurs and business people, to human resource and career guidance professionals and to community groups. Putting aside my thought that 'these people won't be interested in this' (in me!), I discovered that the opposite was actually true. Many of the attendees came up afterwards and declared their interest in learning more. One investment analyst told me "I don't listen and I want to find out how to do that." A real estate agent said, "if this helps with my feeling of being stressed I want to take this course." The director of a community development organization wanted to come into the next course and to have one especially designed for her professional employees. The administrator of a management training centre asked about including the course in their calendar. A professional coach and personal growth trainer wanted to embark straight away on a course to become an Emotional Fitness Instructor. Wow, this stuff works! And this was only a few weeks into my course. In addition, and even more important for me, the opportunity to communicate in a different way with my wife brought an even deeper understanding and love between us in a way that I could not have imagined.

Having now experienced the course 'from the inside' I am more determined than ever to provide the opportunity to teach Inner Balancing to others who are so inclined. This book together with the Emotional Fitness Discovery Manual that is provided to course participants is a major way to take that desire forward and make available what I have learned over the past 25 years. The next stage is to teach Inner Balancing to others who will then be able to bring Emotional Fitness to thousands, rather than the hundreds I am able to reach.

Are you ready to begin the process of becoming an Emotional Fitness Instructor?

You will need to learn Listening Power, which is both the technique of the five-stage process and the art of getting yourself out of the way.

You will learn how to use the Learning from Experience model to help people develop their portfolio of strengths, turning on its head the learning approach used in almost every educational establishment in the world, which is that learners are empty vessels into which teachers have to pour their knowledge.

You will learn the intricacies of the Lifescale and how to engage others in discovering not only their own emotional balance, but how they may change it.

You will learn the Time Capsule and how you can help people rediscover the source of themselves and to communicate in joyful as well as in difficult and always powerfully insightful ways.

You will learn how to facilitate a Group Dialogue and demonstrate to people how they can all tap into their wisdom and achieve positive action in highly supportive ways.

You will learn how to engage others in creating and telling their own stories in Storytime, turning something that may seem tough into enormous fun and release.

You will learn how to help people make sense of their own dreams in Dreamtime, where they will enjoy a journey of a different kind, always within their own control and from their own inner wisdom.

You will learn how to face people with themselves in The Mirror, allowing them to see themselves more deeply than they have done in a safe and supportive environment.

You will learn to conduct the process of Connections where objects and individuals blend into greater insights and understanding.

You will absorb the background of Inner Balancing to pass on to others. You will help others to develop their own Personal Learning Contracts and you will learn how to create your own way of teaching Emotional Fitness.

As an Emotional Fitness Instructor licensed to teach Inner Balancing, you will have access to continuing support, development and training, and to others who are engaged in this work. You will also become part of the development of Inner Balancing, since all those involved as EFIs will be teaching and learning from each other.

Once you are licensed you may set up your own Centre for Inner Balancing and bring Emotional Fitness to all who seek it. You will be giving a great gift to everyone with whom you come into contact, at the same time creating a financially stable lifestyle for yourself.

You will have special qualities. Not many are blessed with the opportunity and abilities to teach Inner Balancing. Use it carefully, maintain your

Without any change we are destitute.

integrity and values, continually enhance your own personal Emotional Fitness training and you will be one of the most valued mentors in your circle.

There has never been more need for people like you to take this out to the world - or at least your corner of it - than there is today. In *Achieving Personal Success* I wrote:

> *"above all else, if we are to survive and develop as human beings in a positive way we need to be heard, understood, accepted and responded to by others as the unique individuals we are."*

In light of what has happened so far in the 21st century those words seem even more significant than they were ten years ago when I wrote them. My hope is that together, through the help of Inner Balancing, we might make a contribution to the emotional fitness of each person on the planet.

There is always another hand.

BIBLIOGRAPHICAL REFERENCES

Berne, Eric. *Games People Play.* USA: Grove Press, 1964.
Cameron, Julia. *The Artist's Way.* USA: Tarcher/Putnam, 1992.
Campbell, Joseph. *The Hero's Journey.* USA: Harper & Row, 1990.
Chopra, Deepak. *How to Know God.* USA: Three Rivers Press, 2000.
Covey, Stephen. *The 7 Habits of Highly Effective People.* USA: Simon & Schuster, 1997.
Erikson, Erik. *Childhood and Society.* UK: Penguin Books, 1965.
Farrell, Warren. *Women Can't Hear What Men Don't Say.* USA: Tarcher/Putnam, 1999.
Frankl, Viktor. *Man's Search for Meaning.* USA: Simon & Schuster, 1963.
Goleman, Daniel. *Emotional Intelligence.* USA: Bantam Books, 1995.
Harris, Thomas A. *I'm OK - You're OK.* USA: Avon Books, 1973.
Heimler, Eugene. *The Healing Echo.* UK: Souvenir Press, 1985.
Heimler, Eugene. *A Link in the Chain.* Canada: University of Calgary, 1980.
Heimler, Eugene. *Mental Illness and Social Work.* UK: Pelican, 1967.
Heimler, Eugene. *Survival in Society.* UK: Weidenfeld and Nicolson, 1975.
Jung, Carl. *Memories, Dreams, Reflections.* USA: Random House, 1965.
Kasper, Jeanette. *Anger is not an Emotion.* Canada: Be You Inc., 2001.
Peck, Scott. *The Road Less Traveled.* USA: Simon & Schuster, 1979.
Redman, Warren. *Achieving Personal Success.* Canada: Merlin Star Press, 1995.
Redman, Warren. *Counselling Your Staff.* UK: Kogan Page, 1995.
Redman, Warren. *Facilitation Skills for Team Development.* UK: Kogan Page, 1996.
Redman, Warren. *Portfolios for Development.* UK: Kogan Page, 1994 & USA; Nichols Publishing, 1994.
Rogers, Carl. *Encounter Groups.* UK: Penguin Books, 1969.
Rogers, Carl. *On Becoming a Person.* USA: Houghton Mifflin, 1961.
Rushforth, Winifred. *Something is Happening.* UK: Turnstone Press, 1981.
Sartre, Jean-Paul. *Being and Nothingness.* UK: Methuen & Co., 1969.

Index

Here's how to contact me:

Warren Redman
Centre for Inner Balancing Inc.
348-5th Avenue N.E.
Calgary, AB, Canada, T2E 0K8

www.innerbalancing.ca
warren@innerbalancing.ca
(403) 245-5463

You may purchase books on-line (ask for discount rates
for quantity), inquire about training opportunities, and
subscribe to our regular newsletters on-line or by mail.
I also encourage you to organize meetings and workshops,
and ask me or another Emotional Fitness Instructor to
speak at your conference.